BARRY LOPEZ was born in 1945 in Port Chester, New York. He grew up in southern California, attended school in New York City and worked in Wyoming before graduating with honors from the University of Notre Dame. His books include OF WOLVES AND MEN, for which he received the John Burroughs Medal for distinguished Natural History writing; WINTER COUNT, a new collection of stories; DESERT NOTES, a companion volume to RIVER NOTES; and now GIVING BIRTH TO THUNDER. He is a contributing editor of *North American Review* and writes regularly for Harper's and other magazines. He lives with his wife in Oregon.

Other Avon Bard Books by
Barry Holstun Lopez

DESERT NOTES
RIVER NOTES

GIVING BIRTH TO THUNDER, SLEEPING WITH HIS DAUGHTER

Coyote Builds North America

BARRY HOLSTUN LOPEZ

A BARD BOOK/PUBLISHED BY AVON BOOKS

Several of these stories originally appeared in other publications: "Coyote Keeps His Name," "Coyote and the Mallard Ducks," "Coyote and the Bear Women," "The Dancing Bulrushes," "The Medicines," "Coyote Visits the Women," and "Coyote Finishes His Work," in *Chouteau Review*; "Fox Loses His Tail," "Whirlwind Woman," and "Coyote Brings a Girl Back to Life" in *Contemporary Literature in Translation*; "Coyote and Wolverine" in *Dalmo'ma*; "Coyote Gambles" and "Coyote Takes Water from the Frog People" in *McKenzie Enterprise*; "Coyote and His Knee," "Coyote Shows How He Can Lie," and "The Tree Holders" in *Skywriting*.

Cover illustration by Tom Pohrt

AVON BOOKS
A division of
The Hearst Corporation
959 Eighth Avenue
New York, New York 10019

Copyright © 1977 by Barry Holstun Lopez
Published by arrangement with Andrews and McMeel, Inc.
Library of Congress Catalog Card Number: 77-17395
ISBN: 0-380-54551-9

The Sheed Andrews and McMeel, Inc., edition contains the following Library of Congress Cataloging in Publication Data:

Lopez, Barry Holstun, 1945—
    Giving birth to Thunder, sleeping with his daughter.

    1. Indians or North America—Legends.
2. Trickster. I. Title.

First Bard Printing, May, 1981

To the Native Peoples of North America

that we may now share a little of each other's laughter
in addition to all our tears

Contents

Foreword

This is not a scholarly book; but then, Old Man Coyote is not a scholarly character. He has consistently evaded academic capture and definition and has tricked nearly every commentator into at least one outrageous and laughable generalization. He is blamed and praised by a wide variety of native tribes for originating death, mixing up the stars, fornicating with birds, bringing fire, losing his eyes, freeing the buffalo; and he is blamed by one anthropologist for nearly putting the American Folklore Society out of business in the 1930s (John Greenway, *Folklore of the Great West* [Palo Alto: 1969, pp. 8–9]).

On the Warm Springs Indian Reservation in central Oregon, some people tell a story about a wandering anthropologist who came across a coyote caught in a trap.

"Please let me out of this trap; if you do, I'll give you lots of money," the coyote said.

"Well, I'm not sure. Will you tell me a story, too?" asked the professor.

"Sure I will; I'll tell you a real, true story, a real long one for your books."

So the anthropologist sprung the trap, collected a big handful of bills from the coyote, and then set up his tape machine. The coyote sat, rubbing his sore legs, and told a long story that lasted until the tape ran out. Then he ran off.

The anthropologist went home and told his wife about what happened, but she wouldn't believe him. When he reached in his pocket to show her the money, all he came out with was a handful of fur and dirt.

And when he went to play his tape for the other professors, all that was in the machine was a pile of coyote droppings.

A person from another tribe might hear this story, smile, and say, "Oh yes, there's that old Coyote up to his tricks again." A Sioux might say, "We tell the same stories about *Iktomi*, the Spider," and the Eskimo would add, "Up our way, it's about the Crow." Only the anthropologist would object, and point out that, after all, these tribes have different and distinct concepts of the Trickster figure and one must not allow the distinctions to be blurred; furthermore, the story as told is recent, an obvious byproduct of acculturation and the attendant breaking down of older traditions. In his zeal for scholarly propriety and with perfectly acceptable academic myopia, the anthropologist might easily and proudly overlook several important aspects of Old Man Coyote: that he is alive and well in the modern world, that he has survived acculturation (and triumphed over it), that—in *spite* of tribal differences—there is a broadly recognizable cluster of characteristics we still know as his own, regardless of our tribal backgrounds. It is this personality profile, and not the scholar's fossil, that Barry Lopez presents in this collection. Say, if you will (and some have), that Coyote is the exponent of all possibilities through whose antics and actions we see ourselves and the moral ramifications of our thoughts; or say that Coyote is the philosophical embodiment of a native world view of relationships between mankind and nature; or say that Coyote is a freak of the primitive mind—the impulsive and self-destructive character that proves the savage did not "have it all together." Or say simply that Coyote is a Gemini. All these things are true; all these things are false.

In spite of my heavy-handed joking about anthropologists, however, I should make it clear that to get *beyond* Coyote's fascinating façade we do in fact need to know his local, specific tribal manifestations. And to know these, we need to know the tribal language, the tribal lore about story-telling events, and the local taboos concerning when a story may be told, by whom, to whom, and under what circumstances. In many cases, the sources of this learning are unavailable to us—some have been destroyed utterly, and those remaining are reluctant to share what there is. But suppose we *could* learn Navajo, for example, along with all the folkloristic, socio-linguistic details we would need to have in mind in order to hear and respond to a Navajo Coyote tale under normal conditions, in its regular habitat. Among other things, we would have learned that Coyote stories must be told *only* after the first killing frost and before the first thunderstorm—that is, in wintertime as defined by nature itself. Knowing that, how could we tolerate the existence of this very book, since it will make the stories available *any* time?

Or, suppose we learn the Coos language, so as to hear of Old Man Coyote in the old, traditional way—only to find out that the stories must remain oral to be alive, that at least two others who know the story must always be present at the telling, and that each tale may be told by a given person only once in the season. Would we not in good conscience refuse to cooperate in the making of this book, or, at second best, would we not at least destroy every copy of it we could find so as to insure that our live oral traditions would not be killed off?

And what will the owner and reader of this book say if a member of some tribe approaches him and says, "Look, in my tribe, all stories are owned by someone, or by some clan. In that book you have there are some stories which were stolen from us, taken and printed without proper permission or ritual. And you are an accessory after the fact"?

Clearly, this is a potentially dangerous book, then, and Lopez has approached the job in the only way I can see as defensible. It does *not* pretend to be an "Indian book." It does *not* provide the original language, the ritual detail, the full context; in short, it does not give away or betray the magic of the actual storytelling event. Instead, the stories are retold in a way that is both faithful to native concepts of Coyote and how his stories should go, and phrased for an audience which reads without listening, for whom literature is studied and reflected upon, for whom Coyote is an imaginary but interesting protagonist.

In these retellings, one important element of style is retained which relates more to the live contexts of the original stories than it does to the tastes of a reading public; a sense of locality, a feeling for place—both geographic and sacred—infuses these dramatic narratives. Small details of geography, seemingly minor references to the color of a feather, the direction of the wind, the smell of grass or water, are all signals which awaken memories, trigger recognition, and allow for the re-experiencing of the texture and quality of a life locally known as it becomes a context for Old Man Coyote's universal adventures. This local perception of region, in all its connotative and sacred aspects, is almost as hard to capture as the Old Man himself. It is well for the reader to know that Lopez has made it his business to spend considerable periods of time experiencing the locales of these stories: he has sat for days in the Oregon desert, listening; he has camped and lingered among the trees and camass prairies of Nez Perce country looking for the spirit of the land; he has gone, and not as a tourist, into numberless reservation towns, Indian bars, and powwows; and he has come face to face with coyotes more than once. He has tried to look and see, not gawk. The result is a sense of what it means to hear of Coyote in different local contexts; this he has tried to incorporate into the style of the tales.

In an exciting article, "On the Translation of Style in Oral Narrative," (*Journal of American Folklore*, 84:331, pp. 114–33), Dennis Tedlock points out that we have ways in our own language of representing the *style* of a narrative done in another tongue. The trick consists in finding equivalents rather than direct translations of connotative words or rhetorical strategies. In effect, Lopez has done these tales over in such equivalent terms, giving us the story, the style, and Old Man Coyote himself, without betraying the magic.

This book is not, however, the collection of dirt, fur, and coyote droppings the anthropologist took home from Warm Springs (where, by the way, anthropologists are no longer a protected species). It is a good Coyote book, with as much of Old Man Coyote in it as anyone has a right to know.

BARRE TOELKEN

Introduction

Those who are familiar with the mythology and folklore of the American Indian know already, perhaps, that Coyote was not necessarily a coyote, nor even a creature of strict physical dimensions. He was known as the Great Hare among many eastern tribes and as Raven in the Pacific Northwest. The Menomini called him *Manabozho*, the Crow *Esahcawata*, the Cherokee *Tsistu*, the Kiowa *Sendeh*. He was Trickster, Imitator, First Born, Old Man, First Creator, Transformer and Changing Person in the white man's translations—all names derived from his powers, his habits and his acts.

No other personality is as old, as well known, or as widely distributed among the tribes as Coyote. He was *the* figure of paleolithic legend among primitive peoples the world over and, though he survives today in Eurasian and African folktales, it is among native Americans, perhaps, that his character achieves its fullest dimension.

In an essay on the psychological roots of the character, Stanley Diamond likened Coyote to a primitive essence of conjoined good and evil; at a time in the history of man when there was no rigid distinction between good and evil, Coyote was. Carl Jung, one of a number of thinkers intrigued with Coyote, wrote that he was "in his earliest manifestations, a faithful copy of an absolutely undifferentiated human consciousness, corresponding to a psyche that has hardly left the animal level. He is," continued Jung, "a forerunner of the savior, and like him, God, man and animal at once. He is both subhuman and superhuman, a bestial and divine being."

Robert Lowie, an ethnographer who worked among the tribes of the northern plains, wrote that Old Man Coyote was "a greedy, unscrupulous erotomaniac." James Mooney, who worked among the Cherokee, called him "the incarnation of the eastern dawn." He wrote that Coyote brought "light and life and drove away the dark shadows which have held the world in chains." The late folklorist Stith Thompson combined these extremes, calling Coyote "the trickster demi-god, a beneficent being, bringing culture and light to his people, and a creature of greed, lust and stupidity."

Paul Radin wrote simply that Coyote was "an inchoate being of undetermined proportions."

As engaging as all these observations are, I think they have served us poorly; they have kept most of Western civilization at too great a distance from the stories themselves. We have come to feel that it is wrong to read without making notes, and our analysis has got us into trouble. We have lost the story in our quest for the character.

Coyote is a creature of *oral* literature and mutable. There are no sacred texts. You can find other versions of the following stories in the pages of academic publications, in folklore archives, in out-of-print popular collections, and in tribal archives. Indeed, I used all these sources (with permission) in preparing this collection (see my bibliographic essay at the back of the book). I took the liberty of rewriting, translating and adapting in the light of this research for several reasons. First, most academic collections preserve to some extent the turgid prose of exact translation, and transliterated prose can be both obscure and misleading in its pretension to accuracy. It is also deadly to read through.

Secondly, to adapt an oral story to the needs of a modern, literate audience does not seem out of keeping with the primary intent of the original storytellers—to engage the listener.

Coyote stories were told all over North America—in Cheyenne tipis, Mandan earth lodges, Inupiak igloos, Navajo hogans and Sia pueblos—with much laughter and guffawing and with exclamations of surprise and awe. This was supreme entertainment but the storytelling was never simply just a way to pass the time. Coyote stories detailed tribal origins; they emphasized a world view thought to be a correct one; and they dramatized the value of proper behavior. To participate in the stories by listening to them was to renew one's sense of tribal identity. For youngsters, the stories were a reminder of the right way to do things—so often, of course, not Coyote's way.

At another level, telling Coyote stories relieved social tensions. Listeners could release their anxieties through laughter, vicariously enjoying Coyote's proscribed and irreverent behavior. Coyote's antics thus compare with the deliberately profane behavior of Indian clowns in certain religious ceremonies. In a healthy social order, the irreverence of both clown and Coyote only serve, by contrast, to reinforce the existent moral structure.

A number of things make this collection unique, which the reader should know. First, it includes Coyote's erotic adventures. Sexual references, as well as stories of cannibalism and bodily functions, were almost invariably expurgated from popular collections in the past, often with a note from the collector indicating he (or she) saw no reason to collect such "off-color" tales for fear of offending the sensitive reader.

Second, just as the deletion of such offensive material projected an unfaithful version of Coyote (one more to the liking of a nonnative American audience) so, too, did inclusion of material restructured for an "and that's why the beaver has a flat tail!" effect. Coyote story collections were sometimes laced with short, explanatory tales of this sort, perpetuating the notion that native Americans were anxious to explain everything, which they were not. Much misunderstanding, in fact, between whites and native Americans was due to white observers striving to make Coyote stories logical or definitive. The reasoning was that you had to have a *purpose* in telling the story—and simple enjoyment or tribal identity wasn't reason enough. Sadly, the juvenile level of some of these popular presentations further encouraged the view that native Americans were shallow people.

A third major difference is the way in which I have treated the hero/trickster dichotomy in Coyote. The dichotomy itself is an artificial one, a creation of the Western mind, but a forceful one. Previous collections have either focused on the heroic aspects of Coyote's character and ignored his foolishness or vice versa. If both concepts were entertained, there was usually an effort to dramatize them singly and segregate the stories by type, often trying to strike a numerical balance. My conscious intent here has been to include stories which suggest the fullness of Coyote's character.

Finally, unlike previous collections which included only a handful of stories told by one person in one tribe, this collection includes stories originally told by a number of people from many tribes, an effort to suggest both the universality of the character and the large number of stories in existence.

These stories were usually told at night during the winter months. They were often related in an animated, prescribed way. The storyteller was not necessarily an old man; it might have been a woman or anyone who could tell the stories well. There were great complexes of stories, some that, strung together, could be weeks in the telling. Other stories were told only once in a person's lifetime.

In the Coyote stories, I think, is more than we, with all our tools of analysis, will ever fathom. We should not feel either embarrassed for it or challenged. To touch them deeply would be like trying to remember the feeling of years of living in the open. We have passed it by, eons ago.

I offer you this Coyote, and I hope something more of the American Indian than we have had until now.

BARRY HOLSTUN LOPEZ

Coyote Keeps His Name

One time Great Spirit called all the Animal People together. They came from all over the earth to one camp and set up their lodges. Spirit Chief said there was going to be a change. There was going to be a new kind of people coming along.

He told all the Animal People they would now have to have names.

"Some of you have names now, some have no names. Tomorrow everyone will have a name. This name will be your name forever, for all your descendants. In the morning you must come to my lodge and choose your name. The first one to come may choose any name he wants. The next person will take any other name. That is the way it will go. And to each person I will give some work to do."

All the Animal People wanted to have powerful names and be well known. They wanted to be the first to Old Man's lodge in the morning. Coyote walked around saying he would be the first. He did not like his name. He was called Trickster and Imitator. Everybody said those names fitted him, but he wanted a new name.

1

"I will take one of the three powerful names," said Coyote. "The Mountain Person, Grizzly Bear, who rules all the four-leggeds, or Eagle, who rules the birds, or Good Swimmer, the Salmon, the chief of the Fish People. These are the best names. I will take one of these names."

Fox, who was Coyote's brother, said, "Maybe you will have to keep the name you have, which is *Sinkalip*. People don't like that name. No one wants it."

"I am tired of that name, *Sinkalip*!" said Coyote. "Let some old person who cannot do anything take it. I am a warrior! Tomorrow when I am called Grizzly Bear or Eagle or Salmon you will not talk like this. You will beg to have my new name, brother."

"You had better go home and get some sleep, *Sinkalip*," said Fox, "or you will not wake up in time to get any name."

But Coyote didn't go home. He went around asking the Animal People questions. When he heard the answers he would say, "Oh, I knew that before. I did not have to ask." This is the way he was. He lost his shirt in a game of hoop and stick, then he went home and talked with his wife. She would be called Mole, the Mound Digger, after the naming day.

"Bring in plenty of wood now. I must stay awake all night. Tomorrow I must get my new name. I will be Grizzly Bear. I will be a great warrior and a chief."

Coyote sat watching the fire. Mole went to bed with the children. Half the night passed. Coyote got sleepy. His eyes grew heavy and started to close, so he took two small sticks and wedged them between his eyelids to hold his eyes open. "Now I can stay awake," he thought, but before long he was asleep with his eyes wide open.

The sun was high in the sky when Coyote woke up. Mole made a noise that woke Coyote. She did not wake him up before this because she was afraid if he got a great name he would go away and leave her. So she didn't say anything.

Coyote went right over to the lodge of Old Man. He saw no one around and thought he was the first. He went right in and said, "I am going to be Grizzly Bear. That shall be my name." He was talking very loudly.

2

"The name Grizzly Bear was taken at dawn," said the Great Spirit.

"Then my name shall be Eagle."

"Eagle flew away at sunrise."

"Well, I shall be called Salmon then," said Coyote in a quiet voice.

"The name Salmon has also been taken," said the Great Spirit. "All the names have been taken except yours. No one wanted to steal your name."

Coyote looked very sad. He sat down by the fire and was very quiet. The Great Spirit was touched.

"Imitator," he said, "you must keep your name. It is a good name for you. I wanted you to have that name and so I made you sleep late. I wanted you to be the last one here. I have important work for you to do. The New People are coming, you will be their chief.

"There are many bad creatures on the earth. You will have to kill them. Otherwise they will eat the New People. When you do this, the New People will honor you. They will say you are a great chief. Even the ones who come after them will remember what you have done, and they will honor you for killing the People-devouring monsters and for teaching the New People all the ways of living.

"The New People will not know anything when they come, not how to dress, how to sing, how to shoot an arrow. You will show them how to do all these things. And put the buffalo out for them and show them how to catch salmon.

"But you will do foolish things too, and for this the New People will laugh at you. You cannot help it. This will be your way.

"To make your work easier, I will give you a special power. You will be able to change yourself into anything. You will be able to talk to anything and hear anything talk except the water.

"If you die, you will come back to life. This will be your way. Changing Person, do your work well!"

Coyote was glad. He went right out and began his work. This is the way it was with him. He went out to make things right.

Coyote Creates
the Earth

Long ago there was no earth, only water. Coyote was floating around on a small raft when he met the ducks. They were the only other creatures. "My brothers," he said, "there is no one else around. It is no good to be alone like this. You must get me some earth so I can make things right."

He turned to the red-headed mallard. "Dive beneath this water and try to bring up some earth. We'll use it as a means of living."

The red-headed mallard dived. He remained down for a long time but came up without bringing any earth.

Coyote turned to the pinto duck. "I sent the older one, but he was not able to get any earth. Now I will let you try." The pinto duck came up after a long time and said, "My brother, I was not able to get any."

"How is that? I thought surely you would bring some."

Then Coyote asked a smaller, blue-feathered duck to dive. "If you do not bring up any, we will have no land to live on." He dived down, but he came up with no earth.

Coyote did not know what to do.

4

Then the grebe spoke up. "My older brother, you should have asked me to go before you asked these others. They are my superiors, but they are helpless." He took his turn diving and stayed down a long time. When he came up Coyote said, "What sort of luck did you have?"

"I have brought some." He had a little dirt between his webbed feet.

Coyote said, "To every undertaking there are always four trials. You have achieved it." Then he took the mud and said, "I will make this into the earth. You will live in the ponds and streams and multiply there where you can build your nests. Now, I am going to make this earth."

Coyote took the mud in his hand and he started in the east. "I will make it large so we have plenty of room." As he traveled along he spread the mud around and made the earth. He traveled like this for a long time, going toward the west. When he had finished he said, "Now that we have this earth, there are some things that want to be here."

They heard a wolf howling.

"Already there is one howling," said Coyote.

He pointed toward the Sun, which was going down, and said, "Listen, there is another one out there now." It was a coyote. "That coyote has attained life by his own powers," said Coyote. "He is great."

Then they all went for a walk. Out on the plains they saw some shining objects. When they got up close they saw that these were medicine stones.

"This is part of the earth," said Coyote, picking up one of the stones which looked like a buffalo, "the oldest part. There shall be stones like this everywhere. They are separate beings."

When they had gone on some ways they saw a person standing near a hill.

"Look," said Coyote, "there is a human being. He is one of the Stars, but now he is down here standing on the ground. Let's go look at him."

When they got up close, the star-person changed himself into a plant. It was the tobacco plant. There were no other plants around at that time. It was the first. Coyote said, "From now on

5

all people will have this plant, take it in the spring and raise it. It is the Stars up above that have come down like this. They will take care of the people. Take care of this plant. It will be the means of your living. Use it in dancing. When you plant it in the spring, sing this song:

Female comrade, the earth, where shall I plant it?"

After that, Coyote found there was no grass. "This is no good." He made it. "Let us make some mountains, hills and trees." He made them all.

He saw there were no fish in the creeks, so he put some there. This is the way he started the whole thing.

Coyote Makes
the Human Beings

One day, long before there were any people on the earth, a monster came down from the north. He was a huge monster and he ate everything in sight. He ate all the little animals, the chipmunks and the raccoons and the mice, and all the big animals. He ate the deer and the elk and even the mountain lion.

Coyote couldn't find any of his friends any more and this made him very mad. He decided the time had come to stop the monster.

Coyote went across the Snake River and tied himself to the highest peak in the Wallowa Mountains. Then he called out to the monster on the other side of the river. He challenged the monster to try and eat him.

The monster charged across the river and up into the mountains. He tried as hard as he could to suck Coyote off the mountain with his breath but it was no use. Coyote's rope was too strong.

This frightened the monster. He decided to make friends with Coyote and he invited Coyote to come and stay with him for awhile.

7

One day Coyote told the monster he would like to see all of the animals in the monster's belly. The monster agreed and let Coyote go in.

When he went inside, Coyote saw that all the animals were safe. He told them to get ready to escape and set about his work. With his fire starter he built a huge fire in the monster's stomach. Then he took his knife and cut the monster's heart down. The monster died a great death and all the animals escaped. Coyote was the last one out.

Coyote said that in honor of the event he was going to create a new animal, a human being. Coyote cut the monster up in pieces and flung the pieces to the four winds. Where each piece landed, some in the north, some to the south, others to the east and west, in valleys and canyons and along the rivers, a tribe was born. It was in this way that all the tribes came to be.

When he was finished, Coyote's friend, Fox, said that no tribe had been created on the spot where they stood. Coyote was sorry he had no more parts, but then he had an idea. He washed the blood from his hands with water and sprinkled the drops on the ground.

Coyote said, "Here on this ground I make the Nez Perce. They will be few in number, but they will be strong and pure."

And this is how the human beings came to be.

The Creation
of the Shoshone

Coyote was out hunting rabbits one day when he saw a very tall woman off in the distance without any clothes on. "Well, I have never seen one like this," he said. "I should go over there and see her."

Coyote went over and began following the woman but he couldn't catch up with her. They walked on for a long time, over many mountains. Finally they came to White Mountain. Coyote was very thirsty by now. He saw that the woman was carrying a small water basket and he asked her for a drink. She gave him the basket jug. He drank for a long time but there was still water in the small jug when he was finished.

They walked on.

Finally they came to a large lake. "My home is over there," said the woman and she began to cross the lake. "I can't do that," said Coyote. "I will have to go around." But the woman turned around and gave Coyote new legs. She gave him the water bug's legs and he followed her over, running on top of the water.

The woman lived with Ocean Old Woman, her mother. Ocean Old Woman had never seen a man before.

The next morning Ocean Old Woman got up very early and began to weave a water jug, a large one.

Coyote stayed with them for some time. At first he had some trouble sleeping with them because they didn't know about that. When he explained it to them they didn't think it was any good, but when he showed them, they liked it. So he slept with both of them.

One day while Coyote was out hunting the two women gave birth to many very small children. They put them all in the water jug the old woman had made.

When Coyote returned they said, "Maybe your brother Wolf is missing you. You should go back home." Coyote said he would go. While he was getting his things Ocean Old Woman spoke to the children in the jug. "You must go with Coyote," she said. "This place isn't your home."

They put the basket of children up on Coyote's back. It was very heavy but Coyote said he didn't mind. He'd carried deer down from the mountains many times.

Ocean Old Woman said, "Now, when you come to Saline Valley pull the stopper out of the bottle, but just a little way. When you come to Death Valley open it again, a little more this time. When you get to Tin Mountain open it again, about half way. When you are in Moapa, open it up all the way."

Coyote said he would do this. At Saline Valley he opened the stopper a little way. Tall, dark people, very good looking, got out and ran away. They were the best looking people in the jug. This frightened Coyote, but he went on. In Death Valley he opened it again. More good-looking people came out and ran away. The women all had long, dark hair, very beautiful. When he came to Ash Meadows, where we are, he opened it up again and the Shoshone people and the Paiute came out. These people were very good-looking too. At Tin Mountain Coyote let some others out but they were not too good-looking. Then at Moapa he opened the jug up all the way and short ugly people came out, very poor. The girls had short hair and lice. They all had sore eyes. The people over there are still like that today.

That's how Ocean Old Woman and Young Woman had the first children. Coyote was the father of everyone.

How Coyote Brought Fire
to the People

In the beginning the animal people had no fire. The only fire anywhere was on the top of a high, snow-covered mountain, where it was guarded by the skookums. The skookums were afraid that if the animal people had any fire they might become very powerful—as powerful as the skookums. So the skookums would not give any of the fire away to anyone.

Because the animal people had no fire, they were always shivering, and they had to eat their food raw. When Coyote came along he found them cold and miserable.

"Coyote," they begged, "you must bring us fire from the mountain or we will one day die of all this cold."

"I will see what I can do for you," promised Coyote.

As soon as the sun came up the next morning, Coyote began the long and difficult climb to the top of the mountain where the skookums kept the fire.

When he got to the top he saw that three wrinkled, old skookums, all sisters, guarded the fire all day and all night, each taking a turn. While one kept watch the other two ate and slept in a lodge nearby. When it was time to change the watch the one at the fire would go to the door of the lodge and call out "Sister, get up and guard the fire."

At dawn the skookum who had been watching the fire all night was always stiff with the cold and she walked very slowly through the snow to the lodge door to call her sister. "This is the time to steal a brand of the fire," thought Coyote to himself. But he knew, too, that he would be chased. And he knew that even though the skookums were old they were swift and strong runners. Coyote would have to devise a plan.

Coyote thought and thought, but he could not come up with any plan. So he decided to ask his three sisters who always lived in his stomach in the form of huckleberries to help him. They were very wise, and they would tell him what to do.

He defecated.

At first, Coyote's sisters were reluctant to help him. "If we tell you," they said, "you will only say that you knew it all along."

Coyote remembered that his sisters were afraid of hail and so he called up into the sky, "Hail! Hail! Fall down from the sky."

This made his sisters very afraid. "Stop!" they called. "Don't bring the hail down. We will tell you what you want to know."

Coyote's sisters then told him how to steal the fire and get it down the mountain to the people without getting caught.

When they had finished talking, Coyote said, "Yes, that was my plan all along."

Coyote then went to see the animal people. He called everyone together, as his sisters had directed, and told each animal— Antelope, Fox, Weasel, Beaver, Squirrel and the others—to take up certain places along the mountainside. When they were all in place, they stretched in a long line from the top of the mountain all the way back to the village.

Coyote climbed back up the mountain and waited for sunrise. The old skookum who was watching the fire had keen eyes and she saw him. But she thought it was just an animal skulking around looking for scraps.

At dawn the skookum left the fire and walked slowly over to the lodge door. "Sister, get up and guard the fire."

Just at that moment Coyote sprang from the bushes. He seized a burning brand from the fire and ran away as fast as he could across the snow. The three skookums were right behind him in an instant. They were so close they were showering Coyote with the snow and ice they were churning up in their fury. Coyote was running as fast as he had ever run in his life. He leaped over cracks in the ice and rolled part way down the mountain like a snowball, but the skookums were right behind him, so close behind that their hot breath scorched his fur.

When Coyote finally reached the tree line, Cougar jumped out from his hiding place, snatched up the fire brand and raced away—just as Coyote fell flat on his face from exhaustion. Cougar ran all the way to the high trees where he gave the fire to Fox. Fox raced until he came to the heavy undergrowth where he gave the fire to Squirrel. Squirrel ran away through the trees, leaping from branch to branch. The skookums could not go through the trees so they planned to catch Squirrel at the edge of the woods. But Antelope was waiting there to get the fire from Squirrel, and Antelope, who was the fastest of all the animals, bounded away across the meadow. One after another, each one of the animals carried the fire, but the skookums stayed right behind them.

Finally, when there was only a glowing coal left, the fire was passed to Frog. Frog swallowed the hot coal and hopped away as fast as he could hop. The skookums were almost on top of him when he dove into a deep river and swam across to the other side. The youngest skookum had already leaped across the water and was waiting for him. As soon as he landed, Frog saw what had happened and jumped between the skookum's legs and bounded away. An instant later the skookums were on him again and Frog was too tired to jump, so he spat the hot coal out on Wood and Wood swallowed it. The three skookums stood there not knowing what to do. None of them could figure a way to take the fire away from Wood. After a while they left and went slowly back to their lodge on the top of the mountain.

Coyote then called the animals together and they all gathered around Wood. Coyote, who was very wise, knew how to get the fire out of Wood. He showed the animals how to rub two dry sticks together until sparks came. Then he showed them how to collect dry moss and make chips of wood to add to the sparks to make a little fire. Then he showed them how to add small twigs and pine needles to make a bigger fire.

From then on the people knew how to get the fire out of Wood. They cooked their meat, their houses were warm, and they were never cold again.

Coyote Places the Stars

One time there were five wolves, all brothers, who traveled together. Whatever meat they got when they were hunting they would share with Coyote. One evening Coyote saw the wolves looking up at the sky.

"What are you looking at up there, my brothers?" asked Coyote.

"Oh, nothing," said the oldest wolf.

Next evening Coyote saw they were all looking up in the sky at something. He asked the next oldest wolf what they were looking at, but he wouldn't say. It went on like this for three or four nights. No one wanted to tell Coyote what they were looking at because they thought he would want to interfere. One night Coyote asked the youngest wolf brother to tell him and the youngest wolf said to the other wolves, "Let's tell Coyote what we see up there. He won't do anything."

So they told him. "We see two animals up there. Way up there, where we cannot get to them."

"Let's go up and see them," said Coyote.

15

"Well, how can we do that?"

"Oh, I can do that easy," said Coyote. "I can show you how to get up there without any trouble at all."

Coyote gathered a great number of arrows and then began shooting them into the sky. The first arrow stuck in the sky and the second arrow stuck in the first. Each arrow stuck in the end of the one before it like that until there was a ladder reaching down to the earth.

"We can climb up now," said Coyote. The oldest wolf took his dog with him, and then the other four wolf brothers came, and then Coyote. They climbed all day and into the night. All the next day they climbed. For many days and nights they climbed until finally they reached the sky. They stood in the sky and looked over at the two animals the wolves had seen from down below. They were two grizzly bears.

"Don't go near them," said Coyote. "They will tear you apart." But the two youngest wolves were already headed over. And the next two youngest wolves followed them. Only the oldest wolf held back. When the wolves got near the grizzlies nothing happened. The wolves sat down and looked at the bears, and the bears sat there looking at the wolves. The oldest wolf, when he saw it was safe, came over with his dog and sat down with them.

Coyote wouldn't come over. He didn't trust the bears. "That makes a nice picture, though," thought Coyote. "They all look pretty good sitting there like that. I think I'll leave it that way for everyone to see. Then when people look at them in the sky they will say, 'There's a story about that picture,' and they will tell a story about me."

So Coyote left it that way. He took out the arrows as he descended so there was no way for anyone to get back. From down on the earth Coyote admired the arrangement he had left up there. Today they still look the same. They call those stars Big Dipper now. If you look up there you'll see three wolves make up the handle and the oldest wolf, the one in the middle, still has his dog with him. The two youngest wolves make up the part of the bowl under the handle and the two grizzlies make up the other side, the one that points toward the North Star.

When Coyote saw how they looked he wanted to put up a lot of stars. He arranged stars all over the sky in pictures and then made the Big Road across the sky with the stars he had left over.

When Coyote was finished he called Meadowlark over. "My brother," he said, "When I am gone, tell everyone that when they look up into the sky and see the stars arranged this way, that I was the one who did that. That is my work."

Now Meadowlark tells that story. About Coyote.

White Crow
Hides the Animals

Out on the plains there was a camp where the hunters were never successful. They could not understand this. Every time they went out to hunt, the game scattered and hid where it could not be killed. This caused the people to starve.

The people did not know that there was someone who went out and told all the buffalo and deer within reach that the hunters were coming and to hide. There was a man in camp who could turn himself into a white crow. He went out and told all the animals to make their getaway. This person, White Crow, would come back later in the day when no one could see him and turn himself back into a man.

The starving people moved their camp in various directions trying to find where the game went. White Crow did not move. Under his lodge was a hole where all the buffalo were. This is where he got his food.

When the people returned to one camp they found this man still living there. He said, "Why did you come back? I have nothing to eat. I have been having just as hard a time as you. I have had nothing to eat since you left."

One day, some of the men were playing a game with sticks and White Crow came toward them. The players smelled the odor of buffalo fat coming from the direction where the man was standing. They noticed that the man had on a good-looking buffalo hide, turned inside out to disguise its newness. He also had a sacred stick rubbed with buffalo fat that they could smell. He did not like their looking at him. He slipped away so they could not ask him questions.

Coyote was there in that village. That night he called the men together and offered to look around White Crow's camp and tell them what he learned. Coyote watched White Crow's camp for a while, then came back and told the men he needed two good men with good eyes. Owl and Dragonfly were the ones chosen. Coyote told them to lie down in the grass and watch White Crow wherever he went. Dragonfly watched so hard his eyes came out. Owl strained his eyes until they became larger than ordinary eyes. Owl watched the man until he saw him go down in the ground.

When Owl came back, Coyote told the men to gather everyone together and announce they were moving camp. Coyote was going to change himself into a little pup and they were to leave him behind. White Crow had a daughter, Coyote told them. "When the people leave she will search the camp for anything left behind and will find me."

The next day, everyone moved and Coyote turned himself into a dog, but he forgot to put on the whiskers of a dog. The little girl found him and brought him to her lodge. When White Crow came in he asked to examine the dog. He saw that there were no whiskers and he told his daughter that he was afraid of this. He said it was a person disguised as a dog. But the girl said she wanted to keep it anyway. She refused to throw it away. She gave it a piece of meat while her father went out to warn all the game to be alert.

One day when the man was gone, the little girl removed the stone that covered the buffalo hole. She called the puppy over to look into the hole but he acted as if he were afraid. "Come over here. Look in here pup, see what we have." When she said this the pup came over. Suddenly he jumped into the hole and turned into a man and began to holler, "Scatter all over the world! Scatter! Scatter!" The buffalo came out of the ground like a big river. Coyote turned himself into a cocklebur and stuck himself on the fetlock of the last buffalo that got past the girl, who was waiting for him with a club. After the buffalo got out of White Crow's lodge and were a long way off Coyote became a man again and shouted "Scatter! Scatter!"

When White Crow returned to his camp and saw what had happened, he said to the young girl, "See what you have done! I was afraid something like this would happen. Now we are going to have a hard time."

Coyote returned to his people and they began to enjoy the buffalo again. This made White Crow angry. He directed the buffalo and the other animals to hide from the hunters. Soon the people were starving again. White Crow let them know he was going to make it harder than before. He flew over the camp saying, "I want you to know it was me who kept you from killing the buffalo before. You are not going to kill meat animals any more."

That night, Coyote called the men together and told them he had a plan. They would have to follow his instructions carefully. They were to announce that everyone should move over to a forest a few valleys away. Coyote would turn himself into a bull elk and hide in the brush where White Crow would not see him. When the people came along they were to kill and butcher him, but they were to leave behind his skeleton and his head with the antlers attached.

So, the next morning, the people moved to where he had directed them and some of them went out to look for game. A hunter scared up the elk, chased him, and killed him. They butchered him the way they had been told.

While they had been chasing him, White Crow had flown over Elk and said, "I wonder how I overlooked you. I should have told you they were hunting and to hide. I am to blame. But you can run fast and save yourself."

After the hunters left, White Crow found the skeleton. He lit on its antlers and thought to himself, "I know this is not an elk. I know what Coyote did before. This is just Coyote, who has disguised himself again. I will test him and find out." So White Crow stood on Elk's head and began to strike at Elk's nose with his sharp beak, saying, "I know you are Coyote! I know you are Coyote!" He kept on striking. He stopped just as Coyote was about to cry out. "Well, I will try another place." He moved back to the hind leg, to the knee cap. He struck with his beak. "I know you are Coyote! I know you are Coyote!" Again Coyote was just about to yell when White Crow stopped.

"Well, you must be an elk, but I do not see how I overlooked you." White Crow then decided he would pick out the scraps of meat left on the ribs. When he stuck his head in between them, Coyote closed his ribs and held White Crow in a vise. Then he got up and turned himself into a man. "Now, I have got you!"

White Crow said, "Coyote, please turn me loose. I will not do anything bad again. I will be good to you all. Please, turn me loose!"

The people were watching from a distance and when they saw that Coyote had White Crow they began to shout.

Coyote said, "Now I have caught you and I am going to take you to camp and let the people do as they please with you." He took him to the camp and the people said, "This is the one who has caused us a lot of misery and starved us. Now that we have him, what shall we do with him?"

Spider Old Woman said, "Let me have him. I want to see the one who has caused us to starve." As she held White Crow, she was entangling him with her web but no one knew this. As she was doing it, White Crow got out of her hands and flew up into the air. He circled the camp, laughing. "This time I will have no compassion on you. This time I am really going to starve you!"

Coyote turned to Spider Old Woman and said, "I am going to tell the people to kill you for letting White Crow get away." Spider Old Woman said, "That White Crow doesn't know what he's talking about. I will get him." She began dragging in White Crow as though she were pulling on a rope. White Crow said, "Hey, I was only joking. I will be good. Have compassion on me." But Spider Old Woman went on pulling him in until she got him in her hands. She gave him to Coyote. "Do whatever you want with him," she said.

21

Coyote ordered the men to go and get firewood. They built a big fire and put White Crow in it until he was burned all black. Then Coyote said, "I am going to make it so you can never do anything your own way. All your life you are going to be a bird flying about looking for scraps. You are going to be frightened by everything."

Now, this is the way with Crow.

Coyote Steals Tobacco
from Crow

Crow had been eating some kind of dead animal. Now he was sitting under some trees smoking his pipe. Coyote was standing a little way off watching Crow smoke. He thought this was very peculiar.

Coyote came over to where Crow was sitting. "What are you doing? I saw you with some smoke in your mouth. Is your mouth smoking?"

"No, that's not smoke coming out of my mouth. It's early morning. You are just seeing my breath."

"No, it's not your breath."

Coyote kept asking Crow what it was until Crow told him. "Well, I'll tell you," said Crow, "I was smoking."

"What kind of plant do you use?"

"I have some over at my house. I have only a little bit with me now."

Crow took up some tobacco and using an oak leaf he rolled Coyote a cigarette. The tobacco was bearberry. Crow had two kinds of tobacco, this kind and another kind he got from some other place. They sat there and smoked.

Crow told him, "Whenever you want to pray you should offer this smoke. This is very holy. The girls like you, too, when you have tobacco."

"Where is your home?" asked Coyote.

Crow said, "I have no home. I live in the tops of the old trees."

Coyote did not believe him. He said, "I know every bird, every person, has a home. Some may live in a hole, some in a cave, some in a nest. But everyone has a home."

So Crow finally said, "Yes, I have a home."

He took Coyote over to his home. Crow showed Coyote his tobacco. "This is real good tobacco," said Crow. Coyote watched where Crow kept his tobacco. They smoked.

After a while Coyote said, "Well, I have to go home. I have many things to do."

He made Crow believe he was going straight home. But he stopped on the other side of the hill and waited in the bushes for Crow to leave.

About noon Crow flew back to where he had been eating the dead animal. Coyote ran swiftly to Crow's home. He went right to the place where Crow kept his tobacco and took it all.

Coyote returned to his camp with Crow's tobacco and began smoking all the time. People came from other tribes to say, "What are you smoking?" He wouldn't say. They asked him for some, but he wouldn't give any away.

The people wanted to smoke, so they decided to play a trick on him. They dressed up a young boy in girl's clothing.

One man came up to Coyote and said, "I will let you marry my daughter, but I will not take a deer for a present. I must have tobacco."

Coyote remembered what Crow had said about how tobacco made you popular with the girls. He was very excited and gave away some of his tobacco.

The people put up a tipi for him. The girl was really good-looking. They said, "You don't have to wait for anything. Just go right in with your new wife."

Coyote hadn't given all his tobacco away so the people came in after him and sat around and asked him for some more. They

24

said, "You are my son-in-law," or "You are my brother-in-law, give me some tobacco," and Coyote had to give them tobacco.

Coyote kept trying to get rid of the people. He told them he had to go hunting early in the morning. But they wouldn't go away.

When the tobacco was all gone they went outside the tipi. Coyote thought they had gone away, but they were close by, listening.

Coyote said to his wife, "You'd better put out this fire and make me a bed. I'm very sleepy."

She wouldn't move so Coyote had to do the work himself. He put out the fire and made the bed.

When they got under the robes Coyote put his arms around the girl. He began to run his hands through her hair and run them down her body.

"You shouldn't do this," she said. "I am menstruating."

"This will not bother me." Coyote fell on her and got hold of her genitals. Then he knew it wasn't a girl.

Coyote ran out of the tipi and called to the people. "You must give me back my tobacco!"

But they had already smoked some of it. Others had given it away. He never got any of it back.

That's how he lost his tobacco. He went away ashamed.

Coyote Brings a Girl
Back to Life

Coyote was very fond of a certain girl whose father was a chief, but both the girl and her father told Coyote to leave them alone. Coyote kept after the girl because he was fond of her, but she wouldn't pay any attention to him. Finally Coyote said he would kill her if she did not become his wife. She told him he could do whatever he wanted, but she would not come to live with him. Her father had told her, "Don't take him. He isn't any good."

Not long after this the girl became sick. Her father was a very powerful man and he brought many medicine men in to cure his daughter, paying them with blankets and beautiful wooden boxes, but they could do nothing and she died. Her people placed her body on a scaffolding wrapped in blankets and surrounded by many presents. Then they went away and mourned.

Coyote heard that the girl had died and he came down from his lodge late one evening. He could see the scaffolding outlined against the sky between the trees. He called, "Get up! Get up!" He heard the body move a little when he spoke and knew he could bring the girl back to life. He took the body down and

26

unwrapped the blankets and mats that bound it. The body only smelled a little. Coyote carried it down to his canoe and started paddling upriver to the place where he lived. When he came to a rapids he got out of the canoe and sang a power song and washed the body in water from the rapids. He did this three more times, singing his song and washing her body in water from the river.

Each time a little more of the smell of the body would be washed away and some color would come back to the skin. Finally, the fifth time, he came to the rapids below his lodge and sang his song and washed her. Her body was warm now and she opened her eyes. "Get up! Get up!," said Coyote. "We are almost home." The girl sat up in the canoe and Coyote reached out to her and fixed her eyes and made her breath sweet.

"Are you awake? Do you know me?" asked Coyote. The girl stared at him. "I am your husband," Coyote said. "After we pass these rapids we will be home. If you ever leave me, you will die again."

The girl thought she had been asleep. When they got to Coyote's house she was very glad because she was very tired. Coyote let her rest but he said, "Remember, if your parents come after you and tell you to come home, you must not go. If you do you will surely die."

It was not long after this that someone who knew the girl came by Coyote's lodge. When he recognized her he asked Coyote if he had brought this girl back to life. He said he had. This was the first time the girl understood what had been done and she asked Coyote if this was really true. He said it was.

The man went back to the village and told the girl's father what he had seen. The chief did not believe this at first, even after he saw that his daughter's body was gone from the burial site. But after a while he came to see things the way the man explained them. He decided he would go up to Coyote's place and get the girl back. So he went with a group of people up to Coyote's lodge and they found the girl there in bed. Her father told her to come home. Coyote was sitting off to one side. He said nothing. The father spoke again, saying, "Come my daughter, we are leaving. You are coming with us."

The girl got up and came over to her father. "Did I die?" she asked.

27

"Yes," said her father. "But that is all over. Now you are coming back with us."

Still Coyote didn't say anything.

"But if I come back with you I will die again," said the girl.

"This is not true," said her father, taking her arm. "Come with me now, we are leaving."

Coyote had said nothing.

The girl led the way out of the house to the canoes. As they pushed off Coyote came to the door of his lodge and called out to her, "Be sure you get a good man for yourself this time. Your father says I am of no use."

When they got home the girl's parents gave her food to eat but she was not hungry. They put her to bed and she went to sleep right away. In the morning her mother called to her to get up and wash and have something to eat, but the girl made no sound and when they went over to her they saw she was dead. Now the family felt worse than before and some of them were angry for what her father had done. They said he should ask Coyote to bring his daughter back to life.

The father sent a message to Coyote, saying "We want you to come and doctor my daughter, for she has died again. If you do this you may have her for your wife."

Coyote told the messengers, "No. Tell him to look for a good man for her. I'm not any good you know. No reason for me to come down."

When the messengers came back with this news everyone said they should offer Coyote a lot of presents in addition to the girl if he would come down and cure her. When the messengers went back and told him this, Coyote said, "I do not want your presents. I will not cure her again. If any medicine man could do what I can do, then people would always be acting like this. No. After this, medicine men can doctor the sick, but they will not be able to do anything for the dead. If people are once dead, they shall remain that way forever."

If her father had acted in a different way, medicine men would be able to bring the dead back to life. As it is now, they can do nothing. Coyote made it this way.

Prairie Falcon Loses

There was a village where Eagle was chief. Coyote was there too. He was a good talker and knew everything. Prairie Falcon was there. He was fierce. The large owl and the small ground owl were medicine men and they lived there too. Panther was there. He was a good hunter. Weasel, Fox and Magpie lived there also. They were gamblers. Many others lived there.

Every day the hunters, Eagle and Prairie Falcon and Panther, went out for rabbits. Coyote brought wood to every house, but he never went hunting. When the hunters came back they gave Coyote the entrails. He took them home and breathed on them and they became rabbits again.

The gamblers played every day at the gambling ground with the hoop and stick.

One day a small, black-eared rabbit came near the village and Coyote went out to meet him. He took him over to Eagle's lodge. The rabbit had food with him, pine nuts and some seeds. He gave all this to Eagle.

The next morning Rabbit went out and began gambling with Fox. Rabbit won everything. He won all of Weasel's beads. He won everything that Magpie had. He won everything the gamblers had. No one had anything left.

Coyote was standing there but he wasn't gambling. He was an advisor.

They stopped gambling that night because no one had anything to bet, but the next morning they started up again. This time Rabbit began gambling with Prairie Falcon. Prairie Falcon won everything Rabbit had. He won everything that Rabbit had won the day before, even the beads that Eagle had given Rabbit for the food.

"I don't have anything left," said Rabbit.

"Play with your ear," said Prairie Falcon.

Rabbit agreed and Prairie Falcon won his ear. He cut it off. "Try with the other ear," he said and Rabbit said he would.

"Wait," Coyote said. "I will be right back."

Coyote went off to Prairie Falcon's lodge where his wife was working on a basket. He changed himself to look like Prairie Falcon. He leaned in the door, "Wife, give me my ball."

"Where is it?"

"It is there by my pillow."

She couldn't find it. "Come and get it yourself."

Coyote came into the house, lifted up the pillow and there was the ball. He pointed it out to his wife and when she looked over he grabbed her and took her down on the bed where he had intercourse with her.

Prairie Falcon began to lose.

Rabbit won everything back again. He won everything he had lost. He won everything Prairie Falcon had to bet.

Coyote came back and asked how the betting was going.

The Medicines

One time Coyote was coming along and he saw a bunch of wild onions. To make them better he sat down over them and defecated. Then he looked them over very closely and said, "Whenever my aunts and uncles, the people, have nothing else to eat, they will eat these wild onions."

This is how he worked.

He walked on a little farther and he heard a voice say, "Everybody eats me."

He stopped and went back to some short grass growing by the river. "What did you say my little brother?" he asked. "Did you say everybody eats you?"

"Yes, everybody eats me."

So, Coyote stooped down and dug up the root and ate it. In a while he began to break wind. At first he thought this was fun. He liked doing it. But every time he broke wind he was going up a little higher in the air. Finally he was going up so high he was grabbing the river willows to keep himself from blowing away. When he began to break the willows off he got frightened. He was going so high now he was grabbing the tops of the trees, but he couldn't hold on to them either. He kept going up higher and higher then falling back to the ground. Every time he fell back he landed on his head.

Finally it was over. He lay down exhausted after he pulled his head out of the dirt. Now when he broke wind it was quiet, only a sound like this, "poo! poo!" When these noises got a little louder, Coyote got scared and ran into a hollow and lay down. He thought someone was shooting at him, but looking around he saw no one. Then he realized it was only himself. He got up and went on his way, breaking wind like that, "poo! poo!."

At the edge of a creek he heard a voice like that other one. "They eat me."

"What did you say, my little brother?"

"They eat me!"

"Well, let me try you."

It was the white root, very sweet. Coyote forgot all about his other trouble and ate it. But the white root was a physic and soon Coyote began to defecate. He defecated until it almost killed him. He had to climb into the trees to get away from the mess he was making. Finally he got on top of a log that projected out over a hollow. He defecated there until he fainted and fell off. When he woke up he managed to crawl over to the river and wash himself off. He wasn't defecating anymore now. He started home.

He had gone a long way and was now out on the plains. Suddenly someone took a shot at him. Bang! He jumped and looked all around. More shots followed. "I am Coyote!" he called, trying to guard himself. But he could see no enemy. He turned around every time he heard the shots, but he could see no one. This went on all afternoon until he had to lay down to rest. At last he guessed what the trouble was. He was breaking wind.

"Well, these little brothers of mine don't agree with me after I eat them," said Coyote. "Now everyone knows."

The Bungling Host

One time there was no food at Coyote's lodge. He went over to see Bear, who always had food.

"Bear, I am hungry, what have you got to eat?"

Bear did not like this way of talking but he asked Coyote to sit down. He said he would make food. He heated rocks in the fire and brought in a large basket of water. Then he cut a strip of buckskin from his wife's dress. When the rocks were hot he dropped them and the strip of buckskin into the water.

Coyote thought this was a silly thing to do. He wanted to tell Bear this was not the way to make food, but he kept silent.

Bear rubbed the cut place in his wife's robe with ashes and it was whole again. When the water was boiling, Bear poured a handful of pebbles into it. Then it was ready.

Coyote thought he would not care for such food, just buckskin and pebbles, but when Bear put it down in front of him he saw that the buckskin had become juicy meat and the pebbles had become huckleberries. Coyote ate his fill and then took the rest of the food home to his family. He told Bear to come and eat with

33

him the next day.

Bear came over. Coyote told his wife, Mole, to put stones in the fire to heat and to bring him a basket of water. He then cut a strip of buckskin from the only robe Mole had and rolled it into a lump as he had seen Bear do. Then he told his wife to put the buckskin and the hot rocks into the basket of water. When it began to boil, he poured in a handful of pebbles.

"Why are you doing this my husband?" asked Mole.

"Oh, you know me, I am always doing this. I am making a meal for our brother, Bear."

While he was talking, Coyote rubbed ashes into his wife's robe, but it did not come back whole again. Coyote shook his head. "I don't understand this," he said. "It always worked before."

When the meal was ready Coyote poured it into bowls. It was still only boiled buckskin and pebbles.

Bear had been very patient.

He reached over and took Mole's robe and rubbed it with ashes and made it whole again.

Then he said, "Coyote, this is my way, not yours. You are not a medicine man, you cannot do these things." Then Bear left.

Later Coyote looked into his cooking basket. It was full of meat and huckleberries.

"Look at this, wife. I have made meat and berries like Bear. What does he know. I am as powerful as he is, he was just afraid to tell me this."

A while later, when they had run out of food again, Coyote went to visit his brother Kingfisher.

"Kingfisher, what have you got to eat," asked Coyote. "I am very hungry."

Kingfisher did not like this rude way of talking, but he sent for his son and told him to go get three willow sticks.

Boy Kingfisher went out and got the sticks and came back. Kingfisher heated them over the fire until they were strong. Then he took them out, twisted them up and tied them to his belt.

He flew up onto the top of his lodge and from there he flew to the river and down through a hole in the ice. When he came up there was a fish hanging on each willow stick.

Coyote ate until his belly was round, but he saved some fish for his wife and his children at home.

"You must come over to see me tomorrow," said Coyote.

"I don't think I will come over," said Kingfisher.

"Oh, you must come over. We will have a nice meal, you will like it. You come over tomorrow."

Kingfisher didn't want to go, but he said he would.

The next day when Kingfisher came over Coyote told his son to go get three willow sticks. When Boy Coyote came back Coyote stuck the sticks in the fire until they were hard. Then he bent them up and stuck them on his belt. Then Coyote crawled up to the top of his lodge.

"What are you doing up there?" asked his wife.

"Why, you know I've done this before. I am getting food for our brother, Kingfisher."

Coyote jumped off the top of the lodge down to the river but he missed the hole and broke his neck and was killed.

Kingfisher had been watching all the time. He walked over to where Coyote lay and took the three sticks from his belt and jumped into the hole in the ice. Soon he came up with many fish. Then he stepped over Coyote four times and Coyote came back to life.

"This is my way, not your way," said Kingfisher. "I do not imitate others like you do."

Coyote took the fish up to his lodge and showed them to Mole and to his children.

"Look at these big fish. I caught them the way Kingfisher did. Kingfisher is afraid of my power. He told me not to do this again. He knows my medicine is strong."

Mole cooked the fish.

Coyote
and the Bear Women

Coyote was walking along the edge of a river and he came on some ripe plums. Farther down the shore he saw a lodge with a little smoke coming out of the top. He picked a few red plums and went over there. There were four women inside with their children.

"Coyote, what brings you over here to see us?"

"Oh, my sisters and nieces, I have brought you some fine ripe plums. I found them up the river, just a little ways from here. I am surprised you didn't see them. They are very good to eat." He gave them some plums and the women thanked him. Coyote made himself at home.

The women were all nursing their children. "Sisters," said Coyote, "make these children go to sleep and I will watch them while you go up and get some more of these plums."

So the women made hammocks inside the lodge for the children to sleep in and put their babies there.

As soon as they had gone, Coyote took the big kettle down to the river and filled it with water and hung it up on a tripod over the fire to boil. While the babies slept he sneaked over and cut their heads off. He put the bodies in the kettle and put the heads back in the hammocks, just sticking out of the blankets a little.

The women came back, bringing many plums in big rawhide bags. "Sisters, while you were gone I went out a little way from here and found a den of gray wolves. I took them out and killed them all. They make very good eating. I have them boiling and they will be ready in just a minute."

The women thanked him for supplying them with all this meat.

"Well," he said, "this has been hard work. I am sweating with all this cooking. I think I'll go outside and cool myself off a little. When the wolves are done you can help yourselves."

Coyote went outside and sat down. He stuck the corner of his blanket back in the door so they could see he was still there.

When the meat was done the women spooned it out. They looked at each other in a funny way but finally began eating.

"Sisters," said one woman, "this meat tastes like our children."

"Oh! Don't say a thing like that. It is a very bad idea to talk like that," said another woman. "This meat tastes strange because it is from gray wolves."

"Surely, Sisters, this meat tastes like our children," said a second woman after a while.

Coyote cut off the corner of his blanket and left it sticking in the door of the lodge and ran off.

After he got a good distance away he shouted to the women, "I have fooled you. You have been eating your own children. I boiled them up and you ate them!"

The women ran to the hammocks but found only the heads of their children. They began to cry and cut their flesh with grief. But these women were bears, too, and they went right after Coyote.

Coyote was running but they were very close to him. He called on his power to make a tunnel he could run into. Just then a tunnel opened up and he ran in and came out the other side and turned around and closed the end up with rocks and brush. Then he put mud over one of his eyes and changed the way he was dressed and went around to the front of the tunnel just as the Bear Women were coming up.

"Hey, Sisters, what is the trouble. What is going on here?" He told them his name was One-eyed Sioux.

"Coyote has fooled us. While we were picking plums he cut our children's heads off and cooked their bodies for us in a kettle. We're after him. He went in this tunnel."

The women were very angry but they were crying, too, and a little out of breath.

"You look tired. Let me go in that tunnel after him while you rest here. I'll fetch him right out. He shouldn't have done this."

He went in but came right out and told the women that Coyote was in there and looked very strong. The women told him not to go in, but he said he would fight him anyway. He went back in the tunnel. The women heard a lot of yelling and howling inside. Finally he came out with his hands and face all scratched up and his clothing torn.

"Say, women, he is a terrible man, but I am going to try again for you." But the women said no, that they had better go in themselves.

"All right," said One-eyed Sioux. "I'll watch right here."

The women went into the tunnel. One-eyed Sioux gathered up a lot of sticks and started a fire at the entrance to the tunnel. Then he heard one of the women say, "I think there is a fire outside."

"No," said One-eyed Sioux, "that is just the crackling birds flying by."

He then put more sticks on the fire which made it smoky in the tunnel.

"I guess there must be a fire outside because it is getting smoky in here," said the women.

"No," called out One-eyed Sioux, "the smoking birds have just gone by."

He was still piling wood up on the fire. The smoke became so thick inside the tunnel that the Bear Women were smothered to death. After he heard no more sounds, he went in and found the four women dead. He brought them all out and cooked them up for himself.

"I was very lucky to find these bears like this," he said to himself. "I like bear meat. You don't find this kind of food laying around. It's work."

Coyote's Son

Coyote was living with two wives. He had a son by the older one and some young children by the younger wife. The young wife was jealous of the older son. She thought he would get the chieftainship from Coyote, so she tried in different ways to tell stories that reflected poorly on the older son. She told Coyote the boy was trying to sleep with her. Coyote didn't believe her at first. He liked the boy very much. But after a while he was suspicious.

One day the young woman went out to hunt for partridge. She asked the boy to go with her but he said he didn't want to. He told her to take one of the younger boys in the village. But she said he was the best hunter and finally he went with her. He shot a partridge for her and then they went back to the village. The young woman pulled up her dress on the way and scratched all around her lower parts until they were bleeding.

That night Coyote wanted to lie down with her, but she said she was too sore. "I'm all cut up from fighting with your son." Coyote looked at her wounds. She said she had struggled with his son in the woods and that he had raped her.

The next day a great crowd of people came visiting in canoes. Coyote was very well known and liked. "My friends," he said, "tomorrow we will go to the islands to collect eggs for my son. We will have a feast for him." Whatever Coyote said, they would do.

The next day Coyote said to his son, "You must go too." "No," said his son. "I don't want any eggs." But Coyote made him go. They paddled toward a big island, Coyote in the back and the son in the bow. "Is that the island?" asked the boy. "Yes," answered Coyote. But even though they paddled hard they never seemed to get any closer. Coyote was blowing on the island when they got near, pushing it farther out to sea. Finally they got there and Coyote and his son began gathering eggs. Then Coyote suggested to his son that he should go inland. "The best eggs are farther inland. Go ahead." When the boy was at a distance Coyote jumped in his canoe and paddled away.

"Father! Father! You are leaving me. Wait!"

"You have been making a wife of your stepmother," said Coyote over his shoulder, and he paddled away. So the boy was left on the island.

One day the boy met a Gull. "Oh, grandchild, what are you doing over here alone?" said the Gull.

"My father left me here."

"You can't get back by yourself but maybe I can carry you over." The boy climbed on the bird's back but he was too heavy. Gull could barely stay in the air.

"Go out to the big end of the island," said the Gull. "There is someone there to help you."

The boy did as he was told. At the far end of the island he found a Fish with two horns on his head.

"Why are you all alone?"

"My father left me here."

"I will take you over to the mainland. Just get on my back and hold on to my horns."

Before they left, Fish asked if the weather was clear. He was afraid of thunder. "Are there any clouds?" "No," said the boy. "Are you sure?" "Yes, I am sure."

The Fish gave the boy a stone. "If you see clouds hit me with the stone and I will go faster. Are you sure there are no clouds?"

The boy said the sky was clear.

So they set out. The Fish moved very fast, but every once in a while the boy would give him a rap with the stone and he would go faster.

Soon it began to cloud up. "Are you sure there are no clouds?" asked the Fish. "No," said the boy, "it is clear." And he hit the Fish again with the stone. The clouds were really coming up now and the Fish thought he heard thunder but the boy said no. Just then they reached the mainland and as the boy jumped for shore a lightning bolt struck and smashed the Fish to pieces.

The boy wandered for a long time. One day he found a lodge. Fox was sitting inside it with a small kettle cooking over a fire. "Come inside," she said. The boy stepped inside. "Grandchild," said Fox, "what are you doing here?" "My father left me." "Well, your father is very strong and clever, but I will try to help you get back. First sit down and eat. You look very hungry."

During this time the boy's mother was mourning the loss of her son. She would go into the woods and cry all day and when she came home at night Coyote would throw burning ashes in her face. Day after day this happened.

Fox guided the boy through the woods toward his village and one day they came to a place where fish hooks were hanging down out of the sky. You couldn't go through there without getting caught. Fox turned herself into a small animal and climbed up into the sky. She jerked the hooks up and told the boy to jump by quickly. He got by.

A little farther on they came to a place where two big dogs were guarding the path. It was a narrow place between high rocks. There was no way to get around. Fox turned herself and the boy into weasels and they began popping up here and there in the rocks and then quickly disappearing. The dogs began barking fiercely at them. They teased the dogs like this until they were frantic and their owner came out and killed them for making so much noise over nothing. Every time he looked in the rocks he didn't see anything.

One night Fox and the boy stayed with two women. Fox warned him to be careful because the women were cannibals. They would try to kill him. Fox gave the boy a knife. That night

41

one of the women got in bed with him. As soon as she felt the knife she got up and went back to her own bed. Next morning Fox and the boy left.

While the boy was coming home, his mother continued to mourn for him. When she went into the woods to cry, some birds would always say, "Mother, I am coming back." At first she thought it was her son and she looked up to meet him, but then she saw it was only the birds. This made her even sadder. When she went home Coyote threw hot ashes in her face. She grew sadder and sadder. When she went into the woods to cry she paid no attention to the birds who were singing "Mother, I am coming back."

One day, after many trials, the boy came near the place in the woods where his mother was crying. "Mother, I'm coming back," he shouted as he came toward her, but she would not look up, thinking it was only the birds. He walked up to her and lifted her face in his hands. "Mother, what has caused your face to be burned?" "Your father did it. He says my son will never come back." "Well, you go to the village and tell Coyote I have come back."

So she went back to tell Coyote.

As she approached, Coyote saw her coming and picked up coals from the fire to throw on her. "Your son will never come back," he cried out. "Yes, he is back now," she answered. Coyote was so surprised he dropped the ashes. When he looked up there was his son.

"You have been cruel to me and to my mother, all for nothing. You left me on an island. I am back. Now I shall be cruel to you. All the days of your life you will crawl on the ground." He turned Coyote into a Frog. Then he said to his mother, "My mother, you shall be the best looking bird in the world. People will never kill you. You shall be the robin." Then he turned his mother into a robin.

Today the frog creeps on the ground and no one kills the robin. Coyote's son did it.

Coyote and Buffalo

Coyote was traveling over the plains and he crossed the mountains and came down on the prairie. There he found the skull of Buffalo Bull. Coyote was afraid of Buffalo Bull but he played with the skull anyway. He kicked it around and threw rocks at it. He spat in the eye sockets and kicked dust on it. When he started to walk away he heard a sound, like thunder. He looked up into clear skies. Then the sound got louder. He turned around. It was Buffalo Bull coming after him.

Coyote ran as fast as he could but Buffalo was right behind him. Coyote felt Buffalo's hot breath on his neck and felt the ground under his feet shaking and he called on his power for help. Just then three trees came up out of the ground and Coyote jumped up and grabbed a limb of the first tree. He climbed up high in the branches. Buffalo Bull began chopping at the tree with his horns. It fell over just as Coyote was able to leap into the second tree. Buffalo Bull charged the second tree and pushed it over just as Coyote leaped into the third tree.

When Buffalo Bull began slashing at the third tree with his

43

horns, Coyote called down, "My friend, please, you must let me smoke my pipe once more. Then I can die content."

Buffalo Bull stopped his hacking at the tree and looked up. "You may have one smoke, Coyote. This is the way for a warrior."

Coyote packed his pipe with fresh kinnikinick and began smoking. After a few puffs, he offered the pipe to Buffalo Bull.

"I will not smoke with you Coyote. You trampled my bones."

"Do not kill me my friend. This is no way to act. Let me come down and I will make you a new set of horns. The ones you have now are cracked and dull looking."

Buffalo Bull let Coyote come down. Coyote took his flint knife and some pitch wood and carved two fine, heavy horns with sharp points. Buffalo Bull liked these shiny black horns very much. As soon as he got them he forgot all about Coyote. He went and killed Young Buffalo with them. Young Buffalo had once taken all of Buffalo Bull's cows. Now he took them back. He liked his new horns so much he gave Coyote one of the cows.

"Never kill this cow, Coyote. When you are hungry, cut off a little of her fat with your flint knife. Rub ashes on the wound. The cut will heal. This way, you will have meat forever."

Coyote promised this is what he would do. He took the buffalo cow with him back over the mountains. Whenever he was hungry he would cut away a little fat and then heal the wound with ashes as Buffalo Bull had said. But after a while he got tired of the fat. He wanted to taste the bone marrow and some fresh liver. By this time he had crossed the plains and was back in his own country.

"What Buffalo Bull said is only good over in his country," Coyote said to himself. "I am chief here. Buffalo Bull's words mean nothing. He will never know."

Coyote took the young cow down to the edge of the creek. "You look a little sore-footed," he told her. "Stay here and rest and feed for a while."

Coyote killed her suddenly while she was feeding. When he pulled off her hide crows and magpies came. When Coyote tried to chase them off, more came. Even more came, until they had eaten all the meat from the young cow and left only the bones.

"Well, at least I will have the marrow," thought Coyote.

Just then an old woman came along. She said to Coyote, "You are a great chief. You should not do woman's work. Let me cook those bones for you."

Coyote liked this woman's attitude. He lay down and went to sleep. When he woke up he saw the woman running off with the marrow-fat and boiled grease. He ran after her but she was too fast. Slowly he went back to his campfire and gathered up the little pieces of bone that were left. He thought he would boil them and make soup, but wen he came back from the creek with water he found all the bones had turned into sticks.

There was nothing to do, he decided, but to go back and see Buffalo Bull and get another cow. When he had crossed the mountains and come up to Buffalo Bull's herd he saw that the young cow he had killed was among them. Coyote said he was sorry, and that he would not do what he had done again. But the cow would not go back with him and Buffalo Bull would not give him another one.

Coyote went back to his village. When he got there he found everyone had moved. They had heard what he had done and were ashamed to be in the same place with him.

Rattlesnake Fools
with Coyote

Coyote was out hunting and met Rattlesnake. They were going along when Coyote said, "Come over to my house tomorrow. We will eat together."

The next morning, Rattlesnake came over. He moved slowly around the floor of Coyote's lodge and shook his tail. Coyote sat over to one side when he heard this. He did not like it. It made him afraid. Finally Rattlesnake settled down.

Coyote put a big kettle of hot rabbit stew down in front of Rattlesnake. "Here, eat, my friend. You'll like this."

"No, I cannot eat this. I do not understand your food."

"What food do you eat?"

"I eat the yellow flowers of the corn."

Coyote was surprised at this but he looked around for some yellow pollen. When he found some, Rattlesnake said, "That's good. Now put some on my nose so that I can eat it." Coyote stood off as far as possible from the snake and put a little on the top of Rattlesnake's nose. "Come over here," said Rattlesnake, "and put enough on my nose so that I can find it." He rattled a little and Coyote jumped back afraid, but after a while he came closer and put some more pollen on Rattlesnake's nose.

When he'd finished eating Rattlesnake said, "I am going now. Tomorrow you come over to my house and eat."

Coyote thought about what Rattlesnake had done and how afraid he had been to get near Rattlesnake. The next day, before leaving for Rattlesnake's house, he put some pebbles in a gourd and tied the gourd to his tail. Then he went on his way, moving on his belly like a snake. This is how he came into Rattlesnake's house, with his hand shaking his tail to make the sound of the rattle.

When Coyote shook his rattle the snake said, "Oh, my friend, I am afraid when you do that." Rattlesnake had a stew of mice on the fire and he put these in front of Coyote, being careful to stay back as far as possible, as though he were afraid to get too close to Coyote. Coyote showed his teeth. Rattlesnake jumped back fast. Then he said, "Please, my companion, eat some of my food."

"I cannot eat your food because I do not understand it."

Rattlesnake insisted, but Coyote refused the food. He said, "If you will put some of the flower of the corn on my head I will eat it. That's the kind of food I eat. I understand that."

Rattlesnake got some corn pollen but he pretended to be afraid of getting too close to Coyote.

"Come nearer, my friend. Put that corn pollen on my head."

"I am afraid of you."

"Come nearer. I am not bad."

Rattlesnake came up to Coyote and put the pollen on top of his nose. Coyote tried to get it with his tongue. But he did not have a tongue like the snake's and he could not reach the pollen. He tried many times, putting his tongue up on one side of his nose and then the other but he couldn't reach the pollen. The snake had turned away to conceal his laughing. Finally, Coyote said he was not really hungry and would eat later. He began to leave and took hold of his tail and shook his rattle. The snake backed off and said, "Oh, my companion, I am so afraid."

Later, Coyote was still crawling along on his belly like a snake. "I was such a fool. The snake had a good stew, lots of it, and I wouldn't eat any. Now I am just hungry."

He went on like that, trying to find something to eat.

The Borrowed Feathers

One day the Bluebirds were busy grinding corn. Coyote came along and said he wanted to grind corn too. The birds knew he didn't know how to do this, but they let him do it anyway.

In the middle of the day it got very hot. "Let's all go up on top of that mesa over there and get a cool drink of water," said the birds. "What shall we do with our friend here?" asked one of the birds. "He has no feathers. He can't fly up there. We must give him some of our feathers." So they gave him feathers and showed him how to fly.

Then they all flew off to the mesa.

"Let's get there before Coyote does," said one of the birds. "He always has some dirty stuff around his mouth. He will make the water bad." They got there before Coyote and had a drink and then Coyote flew in. "Let's take back the feathers," said one of the Bluebirds, "and leave Coyote up here." Everyone thought that would be pretty good. They took their feathers back and left.

Coyote wandered around all day trying to find a way off the mesa. Finally he tried to jump down in one place but it was too steep. He fell to the bottom and killed himself. Later the Bluebirds wondered if Coyote ever got off the mesa and they flew over to see. When they saw he was dead they were afraid he might try to use bad medicine against them, so they made him come back to life again.

They do this every time Coyote is killed.

The Wood-cutting Ducks

In the woods there were some ducks cutting down trees and singing. Coyote came along. He asked them what they were doing and they said they were just cutting down trees and singing. Coyote said he'd like to try cutting down some trees too.

It was hard work. After a while Coyote said he was going to lie down in the shade of one of the trees to take a short rest. He lay down and went right to sleep.

One of the Ducks went over and cut down the tree where Coyote was sleeping. When the tree began falling Coyote heard it and jumped up. He began running for his life but the tree fell down and caught him by the tail. He tried to get out but he couldn't and the Ducks just laughed and flew away.

Coyote pulled and pulled but he couldn't get his tail out. Finally someone came along and took pity on him and helped him get his tail out. When he got free he went off toward his home.

On his way he met a Duck, and Coyote asked him if he was one of those who had been cutting down trees. He said he was.

"Listen," said Coyote. "You are to go to my lodge and find my

50

wife. You tell her to cook you up and leave your head so I can eat it when I get home."

The Duck said he would do this and flew ahead to Coyote's lodge. When he got there he told Coyote's wife that Coyote had said for her to cook up their moccasins and clothes. She started doing this. Then the Duck left. He went over to a pond near some cottonwoods and sat out in the water.

When Coyote came in he asked her where she had put the Duck head. She said she didn't know.

"Did that Duck come, the one I sent to tell you to cook him?"

"Yes, he came, but he told me to cook these things, so I did."

This made Coyote angry. He went out to get some water and saw the Duck sitting there on the pond. He threw his water bucket at him. "There you are! I'm going to get you!" Coyote jumped in and began swimming around trying to get that Duck. But the Duck just flew away.

Coyote
and Sandhill Crane

This happened at a lake. Coyote was going along the shore and saw a bird. He didn't know what this long-legged bird was. At first he thought it was a tree, so he went and sat in the shade it was making. The bird didn't move his legs at all. He just moved his head around a little.

Coyote stared at the bird's foot. He said, "How does this tree stand up? The root is right on top of the earth. And it looks as if it has claws."

A little distance away there was another crane but this one was sitting down. Coyote went over there and asked the crane why he was sitting that way. The Crane had his feet up and his claws out.

"Oh, I sit like this to rest," the Crane said.

"You sit in a queer way."

"That's the way my people sit."

Coyote tried to sit the same way. He sat facing the Crane with his feet up against himself. Coyote didn't like sitting that way. So he changed and sat as he was accustomed to sitting.

Then Coyote said, "You must teach me to sit as you do."

"How can I teach you this? You are a different person."

"Oh, people teach me different things. I can do anything. This should be easy."

"No, I don't think I can teach you."

But Coyote said he could learn so Crane tried. "Stretch your feet close to me." Coyote did this. The bird began to work on Coyote's legs with his claws. He tickled him at the hip.

Coyote said, "Why are you tickling me? Instead of teaching me anything you are making me laugh."

After a while the bird got hold of Coyote's member. Coyote started to laugh. Crane closed his claws tightly and Coyote's face began to change. Very soon tears were coming from his eyes.

"What's the matter? I thought you were laughing. What are you crying about now? Are you crying because you cannot learn my ways easily?"

Coyote was crying because it hurt so much. "I don't want you to teach me any more," said Coyote. "I'm getting tired. I better sit my own way."

So Crane let go of Coyote's member. Coyote moved away quickly. He was afraid to sit close to that bird.

Coyote's member was all swollen. He had to walk with his legs far apart. He didn't want his wife to see him so he stayed away from his home until night.

When he came home he acted in a peculiar manner.

His wife said, "What's the matter with you? Come to bed."

After a while he lay down but he wouldn't let his wife get close.

His wife said, "Let's have intercourse."

"No," said Coyote. "I'm too tired. My legs are too stiff. I've been traveling all day."

His wife tried to tease him and get him excited.

He said, "Don't bother me. I'm stiff all over."

"There's one place that isn't too stiff," she said and she tickled him there.

"Don't! I'm too tired."

So his wife let him alone. When he fell asleep she felt him all over. As soon as she touched that place he woke up. But she already knew what was wrong.

She got after him right away about it. "You have been with

other women! That's what you do every time you go away!"

"I fell on a thorn," he said.

"No, you fell on some woman!"

"I was sitting under a tree and a big bird came and tried to snatch it away."

She didn't believe what he said. She told him, "Stay away from me. I don't want you to sleep with me. I don't want that sickness from you."

So Coyote had to sleep by himself.

Next day he thought he would go see that bird again.

The Tree Holders

Coyote was going along over different prairies and hills carrying his kettle on his back and looking for something to eat. Suddenly he came up on a moose feeding in some willows. He put down his kettle and began tying his hair in knots. He twisted his whiskers up so they pulled his lips out and put a kink in his tail. Then he stepped out into the open near the willows.

The moose looked up. Coyote got down on his belly and began to move backward like a caterpillar, all the time making noises. The moose saw this and began to laugh. Coyote stood up and tried to walk but pretended he couldn't make his legs work. He would go a little way and then fall over on his face. He glanced over at the moose who was laughing very hard now. Coyote tried to make his legs work very fast and go in the same direction but he went every which way and fell over. The moose fell down laughing and died.

"These animals are stupid," said Coyote. "This is the way you have to get them."

He butchered the animal and cooked the meat up in his kettle.

When it was ready he sat down to eat. While he was doing this he heard someone making a noise up above.

"Stop that noise! Don't be noisy while I'm trying to eat." It was only two trees rubbing together in the wind, but they wouldn't stop and Coyote got angry. He put down his food. "You'll have to stop this noise now!" Coyote yelled. But they didn't. He climbed up in the trees and began pulling them apart. But they came back together and pinched him tight. He tried to get loose but he was caught. Just then Coyote saw a pack of wolves coming. He began waving and shouting. "Brothers! Don't come over here! There is much danger. You better go the other way."

The wolves looked at each other. "Perhaps Coyote has something there he doesn't want us to see." They came over and found the meat ready in the kettle. They sat down to eat. That night Coyote was still trying to get out of the trees.

Always-Living-at-the-Coast

Coyote was paddling his canoe down the coast when some people called out to him from the beach.

"Coyote, where are you going?"

"I am going to marry the daughter of Always-Living-at-the-Coast."

"Only a crazy person would do something like that."

That made Coyote angry and he paddled to the shore. He turned all the people into birds and then he turned the flock of birds into deer.

"You will be the deer that men need," he said and departed.

Soon he passed some other people who were standing on the beach.

"Coyote, where are you headed?"

He told them.

"You should watch out then. The bones of those who have tried to marry this woman are piled up high."

Coyote appreciated their concern. He came ashore and put mussels and salmon in the water, which is why you still go to this place for those things today.

A while later some other people called out to him, asking him where he was going. He told them.

The chief then said, "Be careful, Coyote. All my young men have gone there to marry this woman and none of them have come back."

Coyote came ashore and filled the waters along this beach with mussels and gave the people roasted salmon to eat.

At a place called Copper Bottom, Coyote put ashore again and walked through the woods to a village where he saw an old woman steaming clover roots.

The woman was blind but right away she smelled him.

"Coyote! What are you doing here?" she asked.

He reached over and took a handful of clover roots to eat.

"What is this? Who is taking my clover roots?"

"Can't you see?"

The woman explained that she was blind. Coyote then took some pine gum and chewed it and then spit it into the woman's eyes.

"Can you see now?"

"Yes, I can see well."

Coyote told her where he was going. She told him to be careful and gave him some food to take with him.

Coyote went on until he came to a woman working on a canoe. He went over and pinched the feet of her baby. The child began to cry and the woman said, "Do not touch my child. He has never cried."

She went back to working on the canoe, chipping at the inside, but she cut a hole through the bottom.

"Look what you've done. Are you blind?" asked Coyote.

"Yes I am," answered the woman.

Coyote chewed some gum and spat into her eyes. And then she could see.

"Where are you going?" asked the woman.

"I am going to marry the daughter of Always-Living-at-the-Coast."

"You should be careful with her. She has teeth in her vagina. This is how she kills all the young men who come to see her. Take

58

my stone chisel. When you go to bed with her, stick this up in there and break the teeth off."

The woman rubbed Coyote's back with a stone and gave him the masks of the Wren, the Deer, the Mountain Goat and the Grizzly Bear.

Coyote put on a mask that made him look older and went into the country of Always-Living-at-the-Coast where he sat down by a river. He had not been there long when the man's daughter, Death-Bringing Woman, came by with her friends and saw him.

"Oh, he would make a good slave," she said. "Let's take him with us." So they took Coyote back to camp with them. That night Death-Bringing Woman asked Coyote to sleep with her.

Coyote could hear the sound of grinding teeth coming from under her clothes. When he got into bed with her he heard the sound of rattlesnakes. He pushed the stone chisel in and twisted it sharply and broke off all the teeth in Death-Bringing Woman's vagina. Then Coyote took off his mask. He said he was Coyote and he had come to marry her. They slept together.

The next night they arrived at the house of Always-Living-at-the-Coast. That night Always-Living-at-the-Coast heard laughter coming from his daughter's bedroom. He got up from his bed and came into her room.

"Who is that you are laughing with my daughter?"

"This is my husband. Welcome him."

Always-Living-at-the-Coast welcomed Coyote and returned to his room.

The next morning Always-Living-at-the-Coast split some cedar and stripped the bark and made a snare trap. Then he went into his daughter's bedroom and said, "Son-in-law, I want you to jump through that door into the center of the house." Coyote put on his Deer mask and jumped through the door of the room right into the trap, where the Deer died.

"It serves him right, coming into my house and embarrassing me like this," said the old man.

But Coyote took off the mask of the Deer and went back into his wife's room.

That night the old man heard his daughter laughing again.

The next morning he made another cedar bark trap and told his son-in-law to jump through the door into the center of the house. Coyote put on the mask of the Mountain Goat and jumped into the trap where he died at once. When the old man went out, Coyote took off the mask of the Mountain Goat and returned to his wife.

That night Always-Living-at-the-Coast heard the sounds of two people making love again and he called out, "Who is in there with you daughter?"

"My husband," she answered.

The next morning the old man did as he had done before, making the trap and telling his son-in-law to jump into the dimness where it was concealed. This time Coyote put on the mask of the Grizzly Bear and went out into the other room and crushed the trap. Then he sat down to eat.

The old man was still thinking how he might kill his son-in-law. He asked Coyote to go with him by canoe across an inlet to the other shore where they would begin work on another canoe.

Coyote and the old man paddled across the water and went into the woods where they felled a tree and began splitting the log. Coyote took up some alderwood and chewed on it while he worked. They were working along like this when Always-Living-at-the-Coast dropped his hammer into the split. He asked Coyote, who was smaller, to go down in the crack and get the hammer. When Coyote went in the old man quickly knocked out the wedges holding the split open. Coyote spit out the alderwood, which looked like blood, and the old man thought his son-in-law was dead.

"This serves you right for thinking you could come and marry my daughter," he said, and left.

Coyote put on the mask of the Wren and flew up out of the crack. He caught up with Always-Living-at-the-Coast.

"Why did you leave me behind there, father-in-law? The log closed up and I was almost trapped."

"Oh, I am glad to see you. I almost cried myself to death when it happened. I was going home now to tell my daughter. I thought you were dead. I am glad you got out. I didn't think it was possible."

They both got into the old man's canoe and started paddling

toward home. Coyote was chewing a piece of wood. When it was soft he took it out and carved it into the shape of a killer whale and threw it into the water. "You shall be the killer whales of future generations," he said.

Just then the killer whales came up out of the water and snatched Always-Living-at-the-Coast out of the canoe.

When he got home, Death-Bringing-Woman asked him where her father was and Coyote said he didn't know. Later the woman had a son. One morning Coyote took his son and went away.

Coyote
and the Fire-leggings

One day Coyote came on a lodge standing by itself out on the prairie. Coyote looked in and saw a lot of dried meat and other food. Looking around he also found a pair of leggings, made of buffalo hide, decorated with magpie feathers and embroidered with porcupine quills.

Just then Coyote saw the owner of the lodge.

"My friend," he said, "give me these fine leggings."

"No," said the stranger. "I will not give them to you."

"I must have them. I need these leggings."

"They are old leggings. They are of no use to you."

"Well, then let me sleep here. I am tired."

"You can do that," said the stranger and Coyote lay down and went to sleep.

Late at night, when he thought everyone was asleep, Coyote grabbed the leggings and ran out of the lodge. All night he ran until he thought he was too far ahead for anyone to catch him. Then he lay down and went to sleep.

When he awoke a little while later he was back in the stranger's lodge.

"My friend," called the man, "get up and eat." When he saw the leggings next to where Coyote had been sleeping he said, "What are you doing with my leggings there?"

"Oh, I couldn't find anything for a pillow so I just put these under my head." Coyote handed the leggings to the man.

After he had eaten, Coyote decided to stay another night. He wanted the leggings very much and he would try again.

That night when everyone was asleep he grabbed the leggings again and ran away. He ran until morning and then he lay down and went to sleep. When he woke up he was back in the stranger's lodge.

"Here, what are you doing there with my leggings?"

Coyote felt around in apparent surprise and said, "Well I don't know how this happened. I think the leggings like me very much, and they have come over to stay with me."

"Well, my friend, if the leggings like you so much I will give them to you. But these are not ordinary leggings. They are medicine-leggings. You must not wear them every day but only when you go hunting. Whenever you find game in the brush, put these leggings on and run around and around where the game is. This will start a fire and you will easily catch the game. But I must warn you: you must never wear these leggings except when you have a use for them."

Coyote was very happy with his leggings and he started out for home. On the edge of his village he stopped and saw that all the people were watching his approach. He began to dress himself up very fine. "Now, here are those leggings," he said, "I think I will wear them. They will make me look very good."

So he put them on and at the first step sparks flew out and started the grass on fire. This frightened Coyote and he began to run. The faster he ran the more fire there was. The people called out that Coyote was trying to burn down the whole village. At last Coyote got the leggings off. He threw them down on the ground where they burst into flame.

After this, the people in his village looked at Coyote in a strange way, for a long time.

63

The Eye-juggler

One day Coyote was going along and he saw a man throwing his eyes up into a tree.

The man said "Eyes, hang on a branch," and his eyes left him and hung on a branch high up in a tree where they had a good view of the country. When he wanted them back, the man called for his eyes to come back.

Coyote immediately wanted to know how to do this and asked the man to teach him.

The man agreed and taught him, but he warned Coyote not to do the trick more than four times in one day.

As soon as the man was gone Coyote threw his eyes up into a tree. Then he called them back. He could see a great distance out across the land when his eyes were in the top of a tree and he was glad to have learned the trick.

Coyote thought he could do the trick as often as he wanted and on the first day he did it four times. When he said "Eyes, hang on a branch" the fifth time, his eyes went into the top of a tree; but they did not come back when he called them. Again and again

Coyote called, but his eyes stayed up in the tree. Coyote pleaded with his eyes to come down, but they remained fastened to the limb. As the day got hotter his eyes began to swell and spoil and flies began to gather on them.

Coyote called for his eyes to come down all day and into the night, but they never moved. Finally Coyote lay down to sleep.

A mouse ran over Coyote's chest. Coyote was going to brush him away, but then he had an idea. He lay very still. The mouse came across Coyote's chest to Coyote's head and began to cut the hairs on Coyote's head for its nest. Coyote did not move at all. While the mouse was busy cutting the hair, its tail happened to slip down into Coyote's mouth. Coyote quickly closed his mouth and he had the mouse.

Coyote told the mouse what had happened. The mouse said that he could see Coyote's eyes up in the tree and, indeed, they were puffed up to an enormous size. He offered to go up and fetch the eyes for Coyote, but Coyote would not let him go. The mouse struggled to free himself from Coyote's grasp but it was impossible. Finally the mouse asked what he would have to do to go free. Coyote said he would have to give him one of his eyes.

This the mouse did. Coyote took the eye and let the mouse go. The eye was very small and it fit way back in Coyote's eye socket and he could not see very well with it.

There was a buffalo grazing nearby that had been looking on all this time. "This buffalo has the power to help me in my trouble," thought Coyote.

The buffalo asked Coyote what he wanted. Coyote told him he had lost one of his eyes and that he needed another. The buffalo took one of his eyes out and put it in Coyote's other socket.

Now Coyote could see again, but he couldn't walk straight. The buffalo eye was so big most of it was outside the socket. The other eye was rolling around way back inside.

Coyote went around like that, with his head tilted to keep that one eye from rolling out.

Coyote Marries a Man

One time Coyote was going along and he came on a village. There were a lot of people living there and there was plenty to eat so Coyote decided to stay for a while. There was a good-looking man named Not Enough Horses living in the village who wanted to get married but he wouldn't have anything to do with the girls living there. He said they weren't the right kind for him, not good enough.

When Coyote heard this he decided to change himself into a woman and get this man for his husband. He changed himself that way and became very beautiful. He came back into the village on a sled with his tipi and other belongings on it and two wolves pulling it. When Not Enough Horses saw her he liked her right away.

Not Enough Horses told his mother, "My Mother, she is handsome. She's the kind I want. You must invite her over."

The old woman said she would do this. She went over to where the girl was living.

"Niece, you must come over to my house."

"Ho, what for?"

"My son wants to see you."

"I will come then."

"My son desires to marry you," said the old woman.

"You know, so many men wanted to marry me I ran away and came here," said the young woman. "My elder brother said to me, 'Go away'."

"Oh, my son ran away, too, and came here! There were so many women who wanted to marry him. That is why he ran away and came here."

"Oh, that is very interesting," said the young woman.

They went to where the old woman lived and there she saw the young man. He was very handsome. They got married and lived together for some time. Young Woman was a good worker and this made the man happy. Then Young Woman decided to go away. She had had children but she had not let anyone see them. When she left, she left the children behind and when the old woman and her son went in to see them they saw they were wolf puppies.

"Oho!" cried the old woman. "That person was Coyote!"

She was laughing as she wrapped the wolf puppies up in blankets. These were what Not Enough Horses had got for children. All the people in the village were now laughing at him.

They said, "Truly, this is a great thing this man has accomplished. This conceited young man has managed to take a man for his wife! Now we will have something to laugh about!"

They had such a laugh over all this that the young man left the village. He was ashamed.

While he was traveling along he said to himself, "I don't care what sort of woman I marry, what she looks like. Coyote has put me to such great shame."

In a little while he came to a lodge. He stood outside until the woman inside said, "Come in."

"I have come to take you for my wife," he said.

She was too skinny and not good-looking at all. It was dark inside the lodge and he couldn't see well, but he took that woman for his wife. When they slept together he felt very bad because he could feel how bony she was.

In the morning they loaded up her sled with all the things from her lodge and they left that place. They went back toward his village. He was ashamed of the way this woman looked, but he thought at least no one would laugh at him any more for having married Coyote now that he had married this ugly woman.

When they got into the village, his wife got out of the sled. But she wasn't skinny any more. It was Coyote again.

He said, "Hey, young man, are you the same one who married Coyote that other time?"

Everyone in the village began laughing.

Coyote got that young man twice.

Coyote's Member
Keeps Talking

Coyote was out hunting for buffalo, moving through the draws, looking everywhere. Finally he looked over into a little valley and saw some. He jumped down off his horse to urinate before he went after the buffalo.

"Hey, my member," he said, "you see the buffalo over there?" He shook his member at the buffalo.

"Yes."

"Well! You see the buffalo?" He shook his member that way again.

"Yes, I see them."

"Look at that big bull. You see it?"

"Yes!"

"That's a fat bull. Look at it!" Coyote was shaking his member at it.

"Yes, I see it! I see it, I see it, I see it!" said his member. He yelled like that and wouldn't stop. Coyote put his hand over his member but it kept yelling out "I see it!" Coyote began punching his member and trying to choke it but it went right on yelling like that. Finally his member said, "I won't quit until you sleep with your mother-in-law."

So Coyote went back to the village. All the time his member kept saying, "I see it! I see it!"

He stood outside his lodge until his wife heard his member and came out and asked what was wrong.

"I see it! I see it!" said his member.

"I saw some buffalo and was glad and kept asking my member if he saw them until he said he did. Now he won't stop. He said I would have to sleep with your mother before he would stop. Go ask your mother what she thinks of that."

Coyote's wife went and told her mother. She came over in a hurry. "Well, my son is having a hard time there," said his mother-in-law. "Come right inside." Coyote went inside with her. She sang a song and seized his member and cured him.

The Dancing Bulrushes

Coyote was walking along when he heard the sound of a great dance going on. "Oh," thought Coyote, "this is wonderful. I will go to the dance. I am one of the best dancers and they will be glad to have me."

So Coyote hurried on and came to a great crowd dancing on the shore of a lake and he joined in with them. "I am a great dancer," said Coyote. "You will be glad to have me." Coyote was very much taken up with his own dancing and paid no attention to the others.

All day long they danced furiously, back and forth, waving their arms. And on into the night they danced, without stopping, bending and swaying and moaning. When dawn finally came, Coyote was barely able to lift his feet and he was secretly wishing the dance was over.

As the sun rose it became lighter and Coyote discovered that he had not been dancing with people at all. He found himself standing in the middle of a field of bulrushes.

The Deceived Blind Men

There was a large village on the shore of a lake and this village was always in danger of attack by its enemies. Among the people living there were two old men who were blind. The people in the village were afraid that one day the old men would be killed, so they packed up a canoe one day with food and a big cooking kettle and some blankets and they took the two old men to the other side of the lake.

On the other side, the people set up a tipi in a pine grove set back from the water a little ways. So that the blind men would always be able to find the water, the people tied a string to the door of their tipi and tied the other end of it to a post that was standing up in the lake. Then the people left, promising to return to visit.

After that, the two old men began to learn how to take care of themselves. One day one would do the cooking and the other would go to the lake for water and gather firewood. The next day they would switch jobs.

Each evening they divided the meal equally, but both ate from the same bowl, for it was the only one they had.

They lived like this in contentment for a couple of years.

Then one day Coyote came along. He was following the lake's shore looking for crayfish when he came on the line that stretched from the old men's tipi to the post in the water. Coyote had never seen a cord in this place before and he wondered what it was. He followed it all the way up to the tipi.

Coyote approached cautiously and peered in at the entrance. He saw the two old men asleep with their heads at the door and their feet next to the warm coals of the fire. Coyote sniffed and smelled something very good to eat. But he was afraid of waking the old men, so he went off a little way into the bushes to figure out what to do.

A short while later the old men woke up and Coyote heard them talking.

"My brother, I am hungry. Let us prepare some food."

"Very well," answered the other, "you go down to the lake and get some water while I start the fire."

Coyote raced ahead to the water's edge, untied the cord and tied it among some bushes. When the old man came along to get his water he came to the end of the string and dipped his kettle into the bushes. He couldn't find any water. He returned to the tipi and said, "Brother, we shall surely die, for the lake is dried up. There is brush grown up where we used to get water. What shall we do?"

"This cannot be," said his friend. "We have not been asleep long enough for brush to grow up on the lake bed. Let me go."

Before the second man came along, Coyote retied the string on the post in the water.

The second old man entered the lake, filled his kettle and returned to the tipi.

"My friend," he said when he came in, "what you told me was not true. There is water enough. Feel here, the kettle is full." The other one could not understand this at all, and he wondered what had caused the deception.

While dinner was preparing, Coyote slipped into the tipi. When it was ready, one old man placed eight pieces of meat in the dinner bowl and they sat down to talk and enjoy themselves.

Coyote very quietly removed four pieces of meat and he, too, began to enjoy the feast.

"My friend," said one of them, reaching into the bowl and finding only two pieces of meat left, "you must be very hungry. I have had only one piece and there are only two pieces left."

"I have not taken them," said his friend. "I think you have already eaten them yourself." The other denied this and they began to get angry with each other. At this point Coyote reached over and tapped each of them on the cheek. The old men, each believing that the other one had hit him, started to fight, rolling around the tipi, upsetting the dinner bowl and scattering the fire all around. Coyote grabbed the last two pieces of meat and ran out the door laughing.

As soon as they heard his laugh the old men knew what had happened and stopped fighting.

Coyote called out to them from outside, "I have played a good trick on you. You should not find fault with each other so easily."

Coyote went off and continued his crayfish hunting along the shore. Those two old men felt foolish. When their relatives came over they didn't say anything.

The Berries
in the Stream

One day Coyote was coming along and he was hungry. He came to the edge of a stream and there in the water he saw some bright red berries. He dived into the water, right to the bottom of the stream, but he could find no berries.

As soon as he got up on the bank he waited for the water to clear. There were the berries again, right where he'd seen them the first time. He dived in again. He searched the bottom very carefully with his hands but still couldn't find any berries. Now Coyote got angry.

Another time he tried, but no luck.

Finally he thought he had a way to get them. He tied rocks to his legs to make himself heavy so he would stay down longer. He jumped in and searched over the whole bottom but still could find no berries.

He almost drowned before he could pull himself out on the bank where he fell down exhausted. Right there above him he saw the berries. They had only been reflections in the water. Coyote got very angry. He picked up a stick and began to beat the berry bush.

Coyote Builds a Canoe

Coyote was going along as usual looking for some food when he came to a lodge. There were two women inside, an old widow and her daughter, who was very beautiful. Coyote went in and began telling stories, and the widow, who was glad to have a visitor, made a big meal of salmon. Coyote looked around at all the food hanging from the ceiling and piled up in boxes.

When the meal was over Coyote said, "Old Woman, I will marry your daughter."

The woman had heard him tell what a great warrior he was and this made her happy. She agreed.

Later Coyote said to his new wife, "You know I love you very much. I am going to make your mother a nice canoe out of red cedar. Tomorrow I'll go out and look for a good log."

The young woman told her mother about this right away.

The next morning the old woman got up and fixed a big breakfast. When it was ready, she called Coyote and he came and ate. Then he went off to search for red cedar.

Coyote came back just before evening and said he had found a red cedar log that was a good size.

"I will cut it down tomorrow," he told his wife. "Then I will cut it the right length for a canoe."

His mother-in-law made him a big supper.

After he had eaten all he could, Coyote lay down. He whispered to his wife, "When the canoe is finished, we will go for a long trip. You will sit in the stern, your mother in the middle, and I will sit in the bow. We'll have a good time."

The next morning Coyote got up when his mother-in-law called and had another big breakfast. Then he took his mother-in-law's tools and went out. They heard him chopping on the tree all day, then they heard the tree crash and then more chopping.

Coyote came home weary and sore from all the work. He told his wife, "Tell your mother that when I come home at night I want her to boil some good dried salmon. I like this kind of soup. It's good for a man who is working on a canoe."

The old woman cooked like this for four nights. When the fourth day came, Coyote told his wife that the canoe was almost finished. Then he said he wanted to rest and eat for a while because he had been working so hard.

By this time the old woman's provisions were very low, and some of the food boxes were empty.

A few days later Coyote went back to work. He always took along some food for his dinner. Now the old woman was beginning to worry because there was so little food left. She said to her daughter, "Go quietly and see how he is coming along. We do not have much food left."

The young woman went along until she came to where Coyote was. There she saw him standing at the end of an old rotten cedar log, banging it with a stone to make a noise like a man using an ax. There was a large hole in the log and this made a lot of noise when Coyote hit it.

She left and went back and told her mother what she had seen. They took their old canoe and all the provisions that were left and went away.

Coyote came back just before night. When he came in sight of the lodge he was glad and whistled because he thought his mother-in-law would be making a supper of dried salmon. But when he went in he saw there was nothing there. There was just a little fire and some old wooden boxes.

Coyote went on his way again.

Coyote and His Anus

Coyote was going along by a big river when he got very hungry. He built a trap of poplar poles and willow branches and set it in the water. "Salmon!" he called out. "Come into this trap." Soon a big salmon came along and swam into the chute of the trap and then flopped himself out on the bank where Coyote clubbed him to death.

"I will find a nice place in the shade and broil this up," thought Coyote. He went back under some cottonwoods and made a fire and put the salmon on to broil while he took a nap.

While he was sleeping some egg hunters came along.

"Look at Coyote sleeping over there," said Raccoon.

"Hey, look at that big fish he is cooking," said Fox.

"Let's eat Coyote's salmon and broil up his anus in its place," said Wolf.

They went up to where Coyote was sleeping.

"Coyote," said Raccoon, "we are going to eat your salmon, all right?"

Coyote made no answer. Raccoon asked him four times. Finally Coyote made a sound in his sleep. "He says it's all right," said Raccoon. "He says go ahead and eat all we want."

They ate the salmon up, every bit of it, and then they cut out Coyote's anus and put it in the fire. Then they went behind some trees on a hill to watch.

After a while Coyote got up. He could smell the salmon cooking. He went down to the river to wash and get a drink before he started his meal. As he was coming back from the river he noticed that his salmon was gone and he ran up to the fire to see what had happened.

"This looks like something Fox would do," thought Coyote. "It's just like him to steal salmon. But he left this nice piece of meat behind and it might be all right." Coyote took the piece of meat out of the fire. It was just the way he liked it, with lots of grease dripping off it. He began to eat it.

From behind the trees the egg hunters shouted out "Coyote! You are eating your own anus!"

Coyote jumped up. "What was that? I think they must have buried a person alive here once. His spirit is calling out to me."

The egg hunters shouted down to him again, "Coyote, you are eating your own anus."

Just at this moment an ant ran into the space between Coyote's buttocks where his anus should have been. Coyote reached back to scratch but he found nothing there. "I have no anus," he yelled out. Then he realized what had happened. He looked at the piece of meat in his hand. There was almost nothing left. He put the small piece of meat back in place but he had to walk around with his buttocks pinched together to hold it in there. He could hear some people laughing behind some trees and when they slipped off he saw who they were.

"I will follow them and take revenge for this awful thing."

When the egg hunters had finished gathering their eggs, they brought them all down to the river where they dug a pit and built a fire in the bottom. They put stones in the fire to heat, and when the fire burned down to coals, they covered it with twigs and grass and put the eggs in. Then they covered the eggs with a layer of dirt and went to sleep.

Coyote, who had been watching from behind some bushes,

walked into their camp and dug up the eggs and ate all but a few. They were delicious, he thought to himself, almost as good as salmon. He put one egg for each person back in the pit and covered them up. He mixed the last few eggs together and painted everyone's face with the batter. When he came to Fox he shook his head. "You! I knew you'd be here. You are an awful person."

When he was finished Coyote hid in some brush close by.

When the egg hunters awoke, they opened the pit and each one had one egg. "Done just right," everyone said. But when they dug down in the grass and twigs they found only shells. Right away they began accusing each other, pointing to the egg batter on each other's faces. Then they heard Coyote rolling around in the bushes laughing.

"Coyote has done this," shouted Raccoon. "Let's chase him down."

Coyote saw them coming. "Let them come after me," he thought. "I am much too fast. They will just wear themselves out." Coyote went off in a tremendous burst of speed. After a while everyone but Fox had given up the chase. When Coyote saw that only Fox was left, he stopped and waited for him.

"I knew you were in on this, Fox. It's just like you." Fox and Coyote sat down and laughed about what had happened. Then they got up and went off somewhere together. They were good friends.

Coyote and Spider

One day Coyote was coming along. He was very hungry. Spider was on a tree. Coyote found Spider and wanted to eat him.

"What are you trying to do?" said Spider.

"I am going to eat you."

"You know, I heard some people over there talking about killing you. I'll go over there and find out what they are going to do."

"All right," said Coyote. "Come back soon."

Spider promised he would, but he did not return.

Coyote went on and found another spider. He was going to eat him.

"Now, I'll tell you something good," said Spider. "Why do you think I am on this tree? What do you think of this?"

"I don't know."

"I hold on to this tree, shut my eyes for a short time and see everything all over the world. This tree is chief of the whole world, that is why spiders always go on trees."

"That is new to me," said Coyote.

"Don't you wish to see everything?"

"Yes."

"Well, shut your eyes for a while, hold on to this tree, and you will see everything."

As soon as Coyote had closed his eyes, Spider went away. Coyote never saw anything. That's how it was with him.

Coyote and Beaver
Exchange Wives

Old Coyote and Old Coyote Woman lived on one side of the hill and, over on the other side, Old Beaver and Old Beaver Woman were living. They visited each other every night. One night it was snowing hard and Coyote thought, "I'll go over and invite my brother Beaver to go hunting." He told his wife, "I'm going over to see Beaver and tell him we're going hunting. And we're going to make plans to exchange wives, too."

He went over to Beaver's place. When he got there he called out, "Hello!" Beaver answered, "Hello, come in and sit down."

They sat together by the fireplace and had a smoke.

Coyote said, "I came over to tell you we are going hunting. If we kill any rabbits, we'll bring them back to our wives. I shall bring mine to your wife and you bring yours to my wife."

"All right."

"You must go first."

"No," said Beaver. "You go first. This is your invitation. You invited me."

"All right. I'll go early in the morning."

Then Coyote turned to Old Beaver Woman and said, "I'm going hunting for you tomorrow. Then we'll spend the night together."

This pleased Old Beaver Woman. "I'll sing the song so you will kill many rabbits," she said.

The next day Old Beaver Woman began fixing everything for supper and singing the hunting song. She wanted to be ready for Coyote when he got back. It got late and Coyote wasn't back. Old Beaver Woman waited and waited. She was sitting near the fireplace singing,

Old Coyote, Old Coyote, come sleep with me,
Come have intercourse with me.
Ai-oo-ai-oo (making a sound like Coyote makes).

Old Beaver said to her, "What are you singing that for? He won't kill anything. He's no hunter." Beaver Woman waited and waited. Coyote didn't kill anything. He never came.

The next day it was Old Beaver's turn to go hunting. He went to tell Old Coyote Woman to wait for him, that he was going to hunt rabbits for her and then they would spend the night together. "All right," she said. "I'll be waiting."

Old Beaver went out and killed so many rabbits he could hardly carry them all. He came back to Coyote's house that night and walked in saying, "Old Coyote Woman, here are the rabbits!"

She took them and said, "Thank you, thank you Old Beaver."

They went straight into the inner room and Old Man Coyote was left in the front room by himself. Later they all ate dinner together. Coyote was angry. When he finished his dinner he went to bed.

Old Beaver was having intercourse with Coyote Woman in the next room that night and she cried out. "Old Beaver!" yelled Coyote. "Don't hurt my wife!"

Old Coyote Woman answered, "Shut up Old Man Coyote! I am crying out because I like it."

When they were through making love, Old Beaver came over to Coyote's sleeping place. "We want to be friends," he said. "We don't want bad feelings between us. This was your plan. I shall always be at my house whenever you want to visit."

Old Beaver went home. They were as good neighbors as they were before.

Coyote
and Never Grows Bigger

One time Coyote met a very small snake called Never Grows Bigger.

"What a ridiculous thing you are," said Coyote. "Who would ever want to be as small as you are? Why are you this small anyway? You ought to be big like me. You can't do anything if you're that small. There must be something wrong with you."

The snake didn't say anything.

"Let me see your teeth," said Coyote.

The snake opened his mouth. Then Coyote opened his mouth and pointed at his teeth. "See? Look at these teeth of mine. What would happen if we bit each other? Your teeth are too small to hurt anyone, but I could bite you in half. Let's bite each other and you'll see what I mean."

So they bit each other and then Coyote said, "Let's move back a little and call out to each other." Coyote knew that he could tell by the way the snake called out how quickly he was dying. The snake gave a cry and then Coyote called out. Each time the snake called his voice was weaker. Coyote went off a little ways, lay down, and got ready to take a nap. Coyote was still calling out but he could hardly hear the snake. "It's no good to be that small," Coyote thought. "Now he knows."

Soon Coyote noticed that the place where the snake had bitten him was beginning to swell up. The swelling got bad very quickly and Coyote got very weak. He could hardly call out now and he was beginning to feel very dizzy and ill.

By this time the snake's wound had begun to heal. His voice got stronger. Coyote's calls grew weaker and weaker until finally there was no sound out of him anymore. Never Grows Bigger went over to where Coyote was laying down and saw he was dead. "This animal never learns," said Never Grows Bigger. He went away and left Coyote out there on the prairie all blown up like a buffalo bladder from that bite.

Coyote Shows
How He Can Lie

Coyote came into a group of camps. The men were all sitting around. They knew Coyote was always telling lies.

The men called Coyote over. "Coyote," they said, "you are the biggest liar we've ever known."

"How do you know I lie?"

"Oh, you always make trouble and then you lie. You get away with things like that. You are very good at it. Why don't you teach us how to lie so we can lie successfully too?"

"Well," said Coyote, "I had to pay a big price for that power. I learned it from my enemy."

"What did you pay?"

"One horse. But it was my best buffalo horse, with a fine bridle."

"Is that all?"

"Yes."

They did not think that was much, for in those days there were plenty of horses. One man brought out a fine white buffalo horse, his best.

"Yes," said Coyote. "This is a good-looking horse. This is the kind I mean. It was with a horse like this that I paid for my power."

Then Coyote said, "Let me try the horse. If he doesn't buck, I'll explain my power."

They agreed and Coyote got up on the horse. Coyote had never been on a horse before and he dug in with his claws to hold on. The horse began to buck.

"Oh! This horse needs a blanket, that is the trouble," said Coyote.

They put a blanket on the horse.

But Coyote's claws were sharp and they went through the blanket and the horse jumped again.

"Oh! He wants something more over his back. He wants a good saddle on."

So they got a good saddle and helped Coyote put it on the horse. Coyote got on again and then turned his head as though he were listening for something.

"That is my power speaking," he said. "That voice tells me he wants a whip too."

They gave him one.

He said, "I'm going around now and try this horse to see if he still bucks. I'll come right back and tell you about it."

He rode off a little way and then turned around and shouted back, "This is the way I lie. I get people to give me horses and blankets and saddles and other fine things." Then he rode away.

The people couldn't do anything about it. Coyote went home and showed his wife what he had.

"Look at this fine horse," he said. "I took it away from an enemy out on the plains. It was some fight."

But Coyote did not know how to take care of the horse. When he got off, the horse walked away, back to its owner.

Coyote Cuts His Hair

Coyote was walking along the river when he came on some young women taking their baths. They were on the other side and they called out to Coyote, "Brother-in-law, come over and play with us. We would like to have you for a child, one of us at a time."

Coyote jumped across the stream and began trying to fondle the women's breasts.

"What are you doing," they asked.

"I am seeing which one has the nicest breasts. She will be my mother first."

Coyote selected one woman and lay down with his head in her lap. This woman began to pick lice out of his hair, and the other women came around and started picking lice out of his hair, too. Coyote liked this very much. He reached out and tried to grab their breasts and he tried to roll over on top of one of the women, but they pushed him back down.

"You are not behaving like a good child," they said. They pulled the lice from his hair and played with him until he finally fell asleep in the warm sunlight.

When Coyote woke up he was all twisted around. His hair was full of cockleburs. The way they were knotted up in his fur his lips were pulled around to one side of his face and his eyes were pulled around the other way. His thighs were stuck together and his arms were stuck to his buttocks.

Coyote flopped all around trying to get his flint knife out. By rolling over on it he was able to cut away a little hair and free himself. The pain was very bad and Coyote winced as he cut away the hair knots and the burs. He looked awful when he was through, with his hair all cut up.

Coyote started out for his lodge. Just before he came into the village he began crying. When he came up to his lodge he pretended to go crazy. He told his wife how glad he was to see her again. "They told me over there that you had been killed by enemies!" said Coyote. "So I went out and mourned for you. Look how I have cut my hair off short and cut myself all up with my knife. Look at all this bleeding. Oh, how lucky I am you are here."

"Someone gave you false news, my husband," said his wife.

Coyote and Skunk
Kill Game

There was a place where a lot of prairie dogs and rabbits were living. Coyote knew about the place but he didn't know how to get the animals. There was a stream close by. He thought he might change the course of that stream and drown them all.

Skunk lived near the stream. Coyote was walking along there, trying to think how to get those animals, when he met Skunk. He told Skunk all about the rabbits and the prairie dogs. "Let's make a plan to catch them," said Coyote.

"All right," said Skunk.

Coyote said he was going to go upstream a ways and that Skunk should go get some slime grass. The water level would drop off in the stream said Coyote, and Skunk would find him lying in some driftwood. He should take the slime grass, which looked like maggots, and stuff it in Coyote's ears and mouth and all around underneath him, under his tail and in his nose. After he did this, Skunk was to go over and tell all the prairie dogs and rabbits that Coyote was dead.

It was a hot day and as he went along Coyote wished for a

cloud. A cloud appeared over him. Then he wished it would sprinkle so he could run on cool ground. It began to sprinkle. Coyote wished it would rain hard so that the water would come up around his knees, and it did. He wished the water would become deep enough to reach his stomach, and the water came up that far. Then he wished the water would come up so that only his ears would stick out, and the water came up that far. Then Coyote wished he'd be carried downstream by the water, and he was. Then he wished he'd be caught in a pile of driftwood, and he was.

When the water went down Skunk went looking for Coyote. When he found him he put the grass in his ears and mouth and under his tail and in his nose. Then he went over and told the rabbits and the prairie dogs that the person they hated was dead.

Two rabbits came over to see if Skunk was telling the truth, Jack Rabbit and White Rabbit. Coyote had told Skunk to take a stick and hit him in the stomach when the animals came over, so they could see he was dead.

Skunk hit Coyote in the stomach and the two rabbits thought he was dead. They went back and told the others that Skunk was telling the truth. The others did not trust Skunk, so they sent over two other rabbits to see if Coyote was dead, Furry Rabbit and Gray Rabbit. They went over and again Skunk hit Coyote in the belly with the stick. The two rabbits went back and told the other animals that Coyote was dead. But some of them still didn't believe it, so they sent over two prairie dogs to see. Again, Skunk hit Coyote in the belly with the stick. Then the prairie dogs got up close to look at the maggots in Coyote's ears and nose and mouth and in his anus. They returned and told the others. Everyone now believed Coyote was dead.

When the animals arrived, Skunk told them they must dance because their enemy was dead. Some of the rabbits didn't like this and they hung back. But the prairie dogs, they wanted to dance, and started right in. They made a ring around Coyote. Then the rabbits finally came over and started dancing. Soon everyone was dancing. Skunk was singing along with them making a lot of noise when suddenly he said, "Look up there! Look at that pretty bird!" They all stopped dancing and looked up and Skunk turned around and sprayed everyone. The liquid got in their eyes and they couldn't see anything. Coyote had two sticks hidden under him. He jumped up and began to club rabbits and prairie dogs. Only a few got away.

Coyote built a fire and then told Skunk to carry the rabbits and prairie dogs over. Skunk took four big loads to the fire. Then he cleaned all the animals and singed off all their hair. He was doing all the work. Coyote told him to dig a pit and put the animals in with some saltbush. He buried them with just their tails sticking out and built another fire on top of the pit.

While the meat was cooking, Coyote and Skunk sat in the shade of some big rocks. Coyote was thinking. "Cousin," he said, "let's run a race. Whoever wins can eat all the rabbits and prairie dogs. We'll run over to that mountain and back."

"No, I can't run fast at all. Anyway, that's too far to go."

But Coyote kept asking and asking. Finally, Skunk gave in. "All right," he said, "but you must let me start first because I can't run very fast."

At first Coyote said no, but finally he agreed. Skunk said to wait until he got over the first hill.

When Skunk reached the first hill he looked around for a badger hole. He found one and pulled a tumbleweed in behind him. Soon Coyote raced past like he was on fire. Skunk came out of the hole and went back to where the rabbits and prairie dogs were cooking. They were done just right, very tender and dripping with juices. He took them all out of the pit, cut off the tails of the prairie dogs and put them back in the ground so it looked like they were still cooking, and then he went up on a high rock and began eating.

Just as Skunk was finishing his meal, Coyote came back. He was sweating and so out of breath. He was holding on to his knee. He dug up some wet sand in the stream bed to wipe over himself to cool down. "I wonder where Skunk is?" he thought. "He has such short legs, he must be way back there."

Coyote went over to the prairie dog pit and saw the tails sticking up. "They must be done by now," he thought. He reached down and pulled at the tails. "They must be nice and tender. Their tails come right off." He took a stick and dug around in the ashes, but he couldn't find any prairie dogs. He kept digging but there wasn't anything there. He got angry and he began looking for tracks. "Skunk did this," he thought. "When I find him I'll kill him."

While Coyote was running around looking for the right set of tracks to follow, Skunk threw down a piece of bone. Coyote looked up and saw Skunk. "Please, give me some of that meat." But Skunk did not answer. He finished his meal and stretched out for a nap.

Fisher Teaches Coyote
to Make Music

It was winter and Coyote was passing by a lake that was all frozen over. He went out on the ice and walked around. He liked the sound it made when it cracked. While he was walking around he saw Fisher coming toward him.

Fisher had seen Coyote first and gone over to the shore and peeled some basswood bark which he had tied to two stones. He tied one stone to each ankle and came over to where Coyote was. As he walked, the stones bounced on the ice behind him and made a sort of musical sound.

He ran the last little ways to Coyote and Coyote heard the sound he was making.

"Hey, my brother, what have you got that basswood tied to your ankles for?"

"Nothing," said Fisher. "It's just a nice day and I thought I would attach these stones to my legs."

He danced all round Coyote making music, the way the stones fell on the ice. Coyote listened to the ice-music for some time, until Fisher danced out of sight across the lake. Then he went to the shore. He peeled some basswood bark, tied up stones with it and, making two holes in the lower part of his body, he attached them to himself.

As he walked along, the stones made a loud noise on the ice which pleased him. After a while, the stones were making less and less music which caused Coyote to look and see what the problem was. He saw that the stones were far behind him and that he was dragging a part of his entrails on the ice. They had pulled out into a long thing, like a rope. He cut them off and threw them on an elm tree saying, "My nephews, the Indians, will call this the climbing vine. They will use it when they have nothing else for food."

The Offended
Rolling Stone

Coyote was going along one day with his brother Fox and he was feeling good. It was a nice warm day. He came up to a big rock.

"Grandfather Rock," he said, "I am going to give you my fine blanket here. It is too hot for me. You may have it."

He spread the blanket out over the rock and he and Fox went on their way. It was a great blanket of bright beads and porcupine quills, with many small bird feathers that moved in the wind.

After they had gone a ways, Coyote saw a storm was coming up. "I will need my blanket," he thought. So he sent Fox back to get it.

Fox went back to the rock and said, "Rock, Old Man Coyote wants his blanket."

"No," said the Rock, "he gave it to me as a present. I shall keep it. You tell him he cannot have it."

So Fox went back and told Coyote what Rock had said.

Then Coyote said, "My little brother, you go back and tell him again. Tell him I must have that blanket."

So Fox went back to the Rock and said, "Rock, Old Man sent me for his blanket."

Rock said, "No! No! Rocks never give back presents. If you give anything to a Rock, you cannot take it back."

So Fox returned to Coyote and told him what Rock had said.

Now Coyote was very angry. He said, "That Rock has been there for years and years with nothing over him, but now he refuses to let me have my robe." So he rushed up to Rock and snatched off the blanket, saying, "I need this for myself."

Fox didn't like this and he went and hid in some bushes. Coyote went on his way.

Coyote had gone only a little way when he heard something behind him, a rumbling noise. He turned around and saw Rock rolling along, coming after him.

Coyote ran until he came to a den of Bears. He said someone was chasing him and he asked for help. They said they would help, that they were not afraid of anything. Then they asked him what the thing was that was chasing him and he said it was Rock.

"You better go on," said the Bears. "We can do nothing about that."

The Rock was even closer when Coyote got to where Mountain Lion lived. Mountain Lion saw what was happening and told Coyote to pass on; he could do nothing. After a while Coyote came to an old Buffalo bull. When Buffalo found it was Rock chasing Coyote, he told Coyote to pass on.

At last Coyote came to where the Nighthawks were.

"My Grandchildren," said Coyote. "There is a person running after me."

"Hide inside," said the Nighthawks. "We will take care of this."

When the Rock came up it said, "Where is Coyote?"

The Nighthawks gave no answer and this made Rock very angry.

Then the Nighthawks said that Coyote was in their lodge and that they were protecting him. Before Rock could do anything the Nighthawks flew up into the air and dove down on Rock, chipping away at him until he was a pile of rubble.

When Rock was all in pieces they told Coyote to come out and that now he could go on his way.

Coyote went over to the next hill and then turned around and shouted back at the Nighthawks, "Hey, you big-nosed, funny-faced things. You should be ashamed of how you behaved with Rock."

The Nighthawks pretended they did not hear him.

Coyote kept yelling and making fun of them. "I fooled you. I was having a good time with Rock until you lazy creatures became afraid and ruined my game. You have queer-looking heads and your mouths are too small."

The Nighthawks got angry and put Rock back together again and Rock went after Coyote. Coyote tried to get away but he could not. At last he gave out. He jumped over a ditch but Rock was right behind him. Rock fell on him and crushed him.

Coyote Takes
Himself Apart

It was the beginning of winter. Coyote was going along through the mountains and it began snowing. It snowed hard and the snow got deeper and deeper. Finally Coyote couldn't go any farther. Snow was packed on his feet and he was getting cold. There was a big hollow pine tree close by and Coyote crawled inside it. It was warm in there, just the sort of place to wait out the storm. Coyote said to the pine, "Close up! Close up!" and the pine tree closed up around Coyote.

"I will wait in here till the snow settles. Then I will make myself some snowshoes and go on."

But he fell asleep and stayed in there all winter. When he woke up he was hungry. He told the tree, "Open up! Open up!"

The tree didn't open up.

"Open up!" said Coyote. He said this four times but nothing happened. Then he began kicking the tree and abusing it but the tree wouldn't open up.

After a while Coyote heard some people walking by outside.

"Hey, you people going by. I am Coyote. I have given you

everything you have. Open this tree up for me." But they didn't pay any attention.

Coyote kept yelling out that whoever was around should get him out of that tree. Finally Downy Woodpecker landed on the tree and began opening up a hole. All that echoing in the tree from Downy Woodpecker's tapping drove Coyote crazy. "Stop that noise, whoever is doing that. You are giving me a headache."

Downy Woodpecker had made only a small hole. He looked inside and saw Coyote covering up his ears and rolling around moaning in the bottom of the tree. He flew away.

Coyote put his eye to the hole and tried to see if there was anyone coming by who could help him. He looked all around but couldn't see anyone. He thought someone might be hiding close by. "Hey!" he called. "As soon as I get out of here I am going hunting. I am going to make myself a good meal, plenty of good fat meat to eat. Whoever lets me out of here can eat with me." But no one came around.

After a while Yellowhammer came along and began tapping on the tree. He looked into the hole Downy Woodpecker had made and saw the noise was driving Coyote crazy. "Stop making that noise!" yelled Coyote. Yellowhammer kept on tapping. He made another hole bigger than the one Downy Woodpecker had made. Coyote yelled out that his head was aching. Yellowhammer flew away.

Coyote looked out the new hole but he couldn't see anyone. "If anyone is out there, listen. Open this tree up. I will give lots of blankets and warrior's medicine to the person who cuts this tree down." But no one came.

After a while Flicker came along and landed on the tree. He looked inside and saw Coyote, mumbling to himself and kicking the tree. Flicker began tapping. The noise was so bad, echoing in that tree, that Coyote tried to bury his head to get away from it. "Stop making that noise!" yelled Coyote. "I am trying to get out of this tree. You are giving me a headache." Flicker made a hole in the tree bigger than the one Yellowhammer had made and flew away.

Coyote looked out the hole.

"Whoever is out there, open up this tree! I am Coyote. I do not belong in here." But there was no one around.

Finally Coyote decided he would have to cut himself up into pieces and pass them out through the hole Flicker had made. He cut off his tail and threw it out. Then he cut off his legs and threw them out. He pulled out his intestines and threw them out. Then he cut off his arms and threw them out.

Just then Crow came along and began pecking at his intestines. Coyote looked out the hole Flicker had made to see who it was. "Crow, stop that! Those are my intestines." But Crow didn't stop pecking. Coyote yelled at him and called him many bad names, but Crow paid no attention. "These are very good, Coyote," he said. "I don't know why you're throwing something like this away."

Coyote got angry and threw his head out, but before he could do anything, Crow pecked his eyes out. "Why are you throwing these things away, Coyote?" asked Crow. "I have heard you are a great person, very wise, but I don't understand this. This looks like something a crazy person would do."

Crow flew away.

"You are the crazy person," yelled Coyote after him. "I have told you not to fool with these things. Only a crazy person who didn't care about his life would treat a powerful person like me this way."

Coyote put wild rose hips in the place where his eyes had been and then called out "Come together!" and all the pieces of his body came together.

He was hungry and set out to look for some food. He came across a field that had been burned and was still smoking. There were grasshoppers that had been burned in the fire lying all over. Coyote ate them up as fast as he could but they just fell out his anus because he had no intestines.

Squirrel came along. "Coyote, your anus is spilling."

Coyote looked at Squirrel. "What does a person who eats raw sunflower seeds know?" Coyote went on eating.

"Your anus is spilling over, you better take a look back there," said Squirrel.

Coyote turned around and saw what was happening. He took some pitch and stuck it in his anus to keep his food from falling

103

out and then went back to eating. Coyote had to move around carefully to keep from getting burned in that field. He began lifting up logs that were still burning, looking for any mice that might have been caught. He was sending sparks all over when he did this.

After a while Squirrel said "Coyote! Your anus is spilling a lot of smoke!" Just then Coyote felt the heat in his buttocks and turned around to see the pitch had caught on fire. He ran and tried to leap in a creek but he got tangled up in blackberry vines on the bank and burned up.

Where Coyote's food fell out tobacco started to grow.

Coyote Loses Some Blood

Coyote was going through the woods looking for food when he came to where some squirrels were playing. He stood at the bottom of the tree and said, "Grandchildren, you are having such a good time up there and your grandfather is down here starving. Help your poor old grandfather. Give him something to eat."

"No, you are too mean," said the squirrels. "We won't give you anything to eat."

But Coyote kept begging and they finally came down. One of them said, "Now, we will give you something, Grandfather. But you must be careful. This is no time for tricks. You must not cut me the wrong way. Do what I say and you will have plenty to eat."

The squirrel put one foot on the ground and one foot up against a tree. Then he told Coyote to take his knife and cut off one of his testes. As soon as Coyote cut him, down came a lot of pecans, so there was a big pile on the ground. Then the squirrel ran back up the tree.

"Now, Grandfather, you may eat those nuts."

"These nuts taste very good, my grandchildren. But you must take pity on your grandfather and teach him how to do this trick."

"Go on. You can do it the same way, but only three or four times a day. No more."

Coyote went home and told his wife to cut one of his testes off and down poured the pecans. His children all gathered around and ate and when they were finished, Coyote asked if everyone had had enough. They said no. Then he told his wife to cut him again, and again they had a lot of pecans to eat. Four times they did this and then they tried a fifth time. When his wife cut him, this time blood came out but no pecans. This frightened Coyote and he ran back to where the squirrels were.

"Grandchildren! I must have made a mistake. The blood is flowing from me."

"We knew you would not do as you were told. We will stop the blood and heal the wound, but the power will be taken away from you. You are too silly a person to do anything the right way."

Coyote and Mosquito

Coyote met Mosquito and saw that he had a bag on his back. It was filled with blood, for he had been sucking on someone.

"What are you carrying?" asked Coyote.

Mosquito said, "Why, that's blood."

"What are you going to do with that blood?"

"Oh, that's our food. We have no teeth so we have to eat blood."

"How do you hunt? Where do you get blood?"

"When the people sleep, I suck it out."

"How can you suck it out?"

"With this beak."

"Oh, you can't do it with that. You must have some kind of awl."

"No, I've told you how I do it."

Coyote kept bothering Mosquito and asking him again and again. Mosquito kept telling the truth, but Coyote didn't believe it.

So finally Mosquito said, "I carry along a big thorn and I punch the man with it in the hands and face. Then I gather up the blood in this bag when it flows out."

"See! You lied to me before. Now you have told the truth. What do you do with the blood?"

"I take it home and feed it to my little children. They have no teeth and cannot eat anything tough."

So Coyote left Mosquito and went to his home.

He said to his wife, "Give me a water bag and an awl. I'm going to get some good food for the children. They have no teeth and can't eat solid foods." He told his wife, "Some people have killed a few deer and want me to gather up the blood."

It was dark and Coyote who was staying out on the edge of the camp, came into camp quietly. He heard people snoring. He crawled into one of the tipis. It was the chief's. He was sleeping soundly.

Coyote felt over the chief's face and decided on the spot where he was going to get the blood. He stuck the awl into the man's face.

The chief woke up and ran after Coyote. "What did you do that for?" he shouted.

Coyote ran away. He didn't get any blood.

The next morning the people asked each other, "Whose awl is this? Who came around last night?" But no one claimed the awl.

Coyote was looking for Mosquito but he couldn't find him.

Possum Loses His Hair

Possum had a long bushy tail. He was very proud of it, combing it out every day. If anyone came over to his house, he would show off his tail right away. Coyote didn't like this. Everyone laughed at Coyote's tail. They said it was all scratchy and full of weeds and dirt.

One time the Animal People decided to have a council and a big dance. They told Coyote to spread the news. Coyote went by to see Possum, to see if he was going to come to the dance.

"I will only come if there is a special seat for me," said Possum. "It must be where everyone can see my fine tail. I will dance with my tail if you give me a special place."

"You come along then," said Coyote. "We'll have a special place for you. I will even send Cricket over to comb your tail out and dress it all up for the dance." Possum was very pleased with this offer.

Coyote went over to see Cricket and they had a talk. Cricket was the best haircutter anyone knew.

In the morning, Cricket went over to see Possum and told him he was there to fix up his tail for the dance. Possum stretched out and Cricket went to work. When he was all through combing and smoothing the hairs, he wrapped Possum's tail in a bright red string.

"Possum, this string will keep all the hairs smooth until the dance. When you get to the council and it's time to dance then you can take the string off."

When it was night, Possum went to the lodge where the dance was to be and found that the best seat was ready for him. When it came his turn to dance, he loosened the string and stepped out into the middle of the floor.

The drummers began drumming and Possum began singing, "See my beautiful tail!"

Everyone shouted and Possum danced around and around. "See how fine the fur is!" The people shouted more loudly than before and began laughing. "Look how it sweeps the ground!" All the people were laughing now and Possum was wondering what it meant. He stopped dancing and looked around at the circle of animals. They were all laughing at him. Then he looked at his tail. There wasn't any hair on it at all. His tail looked like Lizard's tail. Cricket had cut off all the hairs at the root and now they were scattered all over the dance floor.

Possum was so astonished and ashamed that he didn't say anything. He rolled over on his back and grinned at everyone. Possum still does this when he's caught by surprise.

The Dead Whale

Coyote was having very bad luck hunting. He couldn't catch anything. He was coming along through the woods next to the ocean when he saw a lot of people had gathered around a big whale that had beached on the sand. It was a good fat whale with plenty of meat. Coyote changed himself into a raven and flew over the people, saying "*Gulage, aga dze el ban!*"

The people stopped cutting away the meat and looked up at the raven. They became very worried. Coyote flew around staring down at them.

The next day a number of gamblers got together at one place in the village. Coyote was sitting in with them but they didn't recognize him. He had changed himself. They thought he was a stranger from another tribe.

The gamblers began to talk about what the raven had said the day before. Coyote asked what it was the raven had said. One of the gamblers said, "He flew over the dead whale yesterday in a circle and said, '*Gulage, aga dze el ban!*' He did this two or three times, then flew away to the east."

"Oh, I see, I know what this means. Where I come from we are always talking to the ravens. He was saying 'Maybe a disease will come to this village in a few days.'"

People were troubled when they heard this. The chief sent a crier out to tell all the people they were moving the village. They all got ready and the next morning they moved away.

After that, Coyote made his home in the chief's lodge. He cut up the whale meat and fat and stored it in the other lodges. He filled up the four biggest ones. Coyote stayed around there for a long time eating whale meat and fat.

Coyote and Mouse

The young women were dancing and the young men were looking on. A good-looking young woman there turned to the men and said, "Young men, expose your members." She had told the other women she would sleep with the man with the smallest member. Coyote had overheard this and gone up to Mouse before the dancing started. He said to Mouse, "My dear younger brother, give me your little member. I will give you this fine one of mine. It's what you should have for these women." They changed members. When all the men removed their breechclouts and stood toward the young women, Coyote had the smallest member. The young woman said, "This one is very small, I'll go with him."

But the others said, "Come look, this person's member is enormous! Look at it!" Then they all turned around and saw Mouse coming along dragging Coyote's member. It was taking all his strength. "How is this?" said the men and girls. "Your member is enormous and you are so small. Your member is bigger than you are." They teased him a good deal about it. They poked his member with sticks and swatted it. He tried to get away but the thing was too big. Finally he said, "This is not mine!"

"Whose is it?"

"It is First Worker's. He took mine off with him, this is his. I'm trying to walk with it. It's no use. I can't even drag it."

They called out, "First Worker, you wished to get that girl. You took this person's member. Come on, this is your member. Take it back." Coyote came over. He saw his member was all covered with dust and cuts. He said to the mouse, "Let's go." They went over into a gully and he took back his organ. He knocked the mouse down and went away.

The Sharpened Leg

There was a man whose leg was pointed, so he could run and jump and stick himself in the side of a tree. By saying, "Leg come out" he brought himself back to the ground. On a hot day he would put himself high up in a tree where there was shade and a good breeze. But he could not do this trick more than four times in one day.

Once, while he was doing this trick, Coyote came along.

"Hey, my Brother, what is this you are doing?"

"I am getting up in the shade of this tree, out of the heat."

"Sharpen my leg. Then I can do that too," said Coyote.

Coyote stood up on a log while the man sharpened his leg with an ax. It hurt and the tears were coming down Coyote's face.

When he was through the man told Coyote to only do this trick four times a day. He told him to keep count so he would not do it more than four times.

Coyote said he would and went off toward the river, singing one of his songs. When he got there he threw himself up in a large cottonwood tree and stuck in the bark. Then he called himself

115

back to the ground. "I was only testing this trick," said Coyote to himself. "Now I will start counting." He ran at a tree and jumped and stuck himself in the side of it and counted "One!"

The next time he jumped he shouted "Two!"

The next time he counted "Three!" and stuck way up in the branches of a pine tree.

By this time there were many animals standing around watching what Coyote did. They asked him to teach them this trick. "Where did you learn that?" they asked. Coyote walked around very proud. He wouldn't say.

Finally a fifth time he ran at a tree, jumped up as high as he could and stuck his leg in up to the thigh. Everyone looked at each other. This was very powerful, what Coyote was doing. Then Coyote yelled, "Leg come out!" to get back to the ground, but nothing happened. He called out again, "Leg come out!" but he was stuck. He told the animals who were watching to go find the man who had taught him this trick and bring him back, but they just walked away. They knew now it was just Coyote. He stayed stuck in that tree until he starved to death.

Coyote and Wolverine

One time Coyote's wife had a lover named Wolverine, but Coyote didn't know about it. He and his wife were out hunting one day when they came on Wolverine's lodge. They went inside. Wolverine was alarmed but Coyote didn't know who the man was.

"What are you hunting?" said Wolverine, looking at Coyote's weapons.

"Oh, anything that I see. I hunt whatever I can get."

"What are you hunting now," asked Wolverine. He was anxious to see if Coyote knew about his sleeping with his wife. He kept putting the question to Coyote until Coyote said, "I am hunting Wolverine" in order to shut him up.

This frightened Wolverine, and he went outside his lodge. Coyote and his wife came out too. They went down by the water where Wolverine was standing.

"I think my canoe is longer than yours," said Wolverine. "Pull your canoe over and let's measure and see."

Coyote got his canoe and pushed it over to where Wolverine

117

was. They were putting their canoes together to see which one was the longest when suddenly Wolverine grabbed Coyote's wife, jumped into his canoe and paddled away. Coyote went after them and was about to catch up when Wolverine brought a fog down and Coyote got lost. He paddled around and around, but he could find no trace of his wife. Finally he gave up and paddled home.

He was very sad. Coyote lay under his blanket for a long time wondering how to get his wife back. Finally he went down to his canoe and asked his canoe paddle where his wife was. The canoe paddle answered, but with a mumbling voice, so Coyote couldn't understand what it was saying. He grabbed the paddle and said he would break it in half if it did not speak in a way he could understand. The canoe paddle went on mumbling. Coyote took it over his knee and bent it until it almost broke he was so angry. But the canoe paddle kept mumbling in the same way and Coyote threw it in the bottom of the canoe.

He went back and lay down under his blanket and thought about the whole thing again and, when he had thought it through, he went back to his canoe and asked the paddle where his wife was. Finally he understood the paddle. The paddle told him his wife was in a village called Clouds Laying Down, on a big lake to the north.

Coyote spent one whole day defecating around the shore. From all this excrement he made warriors and canoes. His friends Marten and Fisher joined him and one morning they all set out.

When they came to Clouds Laying Down they saw a long house in the fog and they put ashore and went inside. All the people of the village were in there. They looked out between the logs at the other warriors, sitting in their canoes in the fog on the lake.

While they were sitting there Marten and Fisher began walking around on the ceiling of the lodge and walking across the walls. The people wondered at this and asked Coyote how it was done. Coyote said he gave Marten and Fisher this power by cutting out their intestines and defecating in the cavity. This made them light enough to go anywhere. Some of the people said they wanted this power but Coyote said he couldn't give it to just a few people.

He would have to give it to everyone or to no one. All the men decided they wanted this power, to be able to walk around anywhere. Coyote told them to come and line up on the beach. When they had lined up he walked along and disemboweled each one. When he was finished, they were all dead. Wolverine was among them. Coyote took his wife and went back to the place where he lived.

Coyote and the
Bad-medicine Woman

Coyote was coming along a trail between two villages when he saw a bad-medicine woman. He grabbed his hair and pulled it down so it was very long and looked good.

When they met, the bad-medicine woman asked him, "How do you get your hair to be this long and to look so fine?"

"It is not hard. I look for a tree that is bent over and then I climb up and tie my hair on a limb and jump down."

After Coyote went on the old woman went looking for a tree that was bent over. She found one and climbed up and tied her hair in the branches. Then she jumped. Her hair stayed in the tree.

When she recovered her senses she was just in time to see a buzzard going after her scalp up in the tree. She got up there in a hurry to get it back. "Coyote!" she screamed. "You trickster. You have cheated me badly. It is the last time."

She rubbed some spittle on her head and put her scalp back on.

A few days later Coyote saw the bad-medicine woman coming along and he covered himself all over with different colored paints.

When they met, the old woman asked, "My friend, how did you get those nice stripes all over your body? I would like some just like this. How do you do it?"

"Oh, it is very easy. First you dig a hole in the ground, down as far as you can reach. Then build a fire in there. When the coals are hot spread them around evenly. Then wrap yourself in freshly peeled bark and roll over on those coals. That's the way to get these stripes."

The old woman went out and began to gather dry branches for the fire. She dug the trench and got a good bed of hot coals spread out. Then she wrapped herself in freshly peeled bark and lay down on the fire. She rolled over a few times but she had a hard time getting out of the hole.

She was burned all over. When she took off the bark it pulled patches of her skin off. She had nothing but blisters. Coyote was right there laughing. "Coyote!" she yelled out. "You trickster. You've done this again. But this is the last time."

A little while later Coyote was coming along and he saw the old woman again. He changed himself around so she would not know him. One of the things he did was replace his eyes with plum stones.

When Bad-medicine Woman saw these stones she couldn't help herself. "My friend, how did it happen that you have such fine eyes?"

"It is very simple. I just replace my eyes."

"Oh, they are beautiful. I must have eyes like this."

Coyote said he would do this for her. He plucked her eyes out and put in the plum stones.

"There. Now you look good. Look over there."

The old woman turned her head.

"You see the woods over there?"

"Oh yes! I see them far better than I did even when I was a young woman."

But she couldn't see anything. She walked into a tree and fell down. Coyote began laughing. She heard this but she didn't say anything. She just got some mud-sticking birds to go find her eyes for her and put them back in. That was Bad-medicine Woman.

Coyote and Rabbit

Once when Coyote was coming along he found Rabbit making a sack.

"What is this sack for, Rabbit?"

"I am making this sack to keep myself from being killed when the hailstorm comes this afternoon."

"My friend, you are very good at this. You make fine sacks. Give me this one and make another one for yourself."

Coyote got into the bag and Rabbit hung him in a tree where he would be safe. Then Rabbit yelled as though the hail were coming and he began pelting Coyote with rocks. Coyote was in great pain but he put up with it. Finally he fell from the tree and got his head out of the bag and saw that it was only Rabbit throwing rocks at him.

Rabbit ran off. Coyote was very angry and when he got out of the bag he chased after Rabbit.

Coyote found Rabbit lying down chewing on some soft gum. He said, "What are you chewing? What is this for?"

"It will be very hot today," said Rabbit. "I am chewing this gum to make spectacles to protect my eyes. Otherwise the sun will hurt them."

"Let me have this pair. You know how to make them. You can make yourself another pair."

"Very well," said Rabbit and gave the eye-shields to Coyote.

Rabbit adjusted the eye-shields until Coyote could not see anything at all. Then he set fire to the brush all around Coyote and ran off. Coyote got his fur badly singed in the fire and the gum melted all over his face and stuck in his hair.

He started out to catch Rabbit again and said he would kill him as soon as he saw him.

When he found him, Rabbit was sitting in front of a beehive.

"Rabbit, I am going to kill you."

"You must not kill me. I am teaching these children."

The hive was closed and Coyote could not see into it.

"Who is in there?"

"If you wish to see inside you must teach for a while while I take a rest. When it is dinner time you must hit the hive with this club until they come out. Just keep hitting. They don't hear very well."

Coyote sat there for a long time telling the people he thought were in the hive all about the times he had been in battle and what a great warrior he was. When dinner time came he hit the hive so hard it broke in two. The bees came out and stung him all over until he was all puffed up.

"I'm going to kill you before you can say another word," he yelled and ran after Rabbit. He was so mad he was biting his tongue and walking into rocks.

Rabbit came to a field of watermelons. In the middle of the field there was a stick figure made of gum. Rabbit hit it with his foot and got stuck. He got his other foot stuck, then one hand and then his other hand and finally his head. This is how Coyote found him.

"What are you doing like this?" asked Coyote.

"The farmer who owns this melon patch was mad because I would not eat melons with him. He stuck me on here and said that in a while he would make me eat chicken with him. I told him I wouldn't do it."

123

"You are foolish. I will take your place."

Coyote pulled Rabbit free and stuck himself up in the gum trap. When the farmer who owned the melons came out and saw Coyote he shot him full of holes.

Whirlwind Woman

Coyote was traveling. He met Whirlwind Woman who sometimes crawled along in the shape of a caterpillar. "Get out of my
way," said Coyote. Whirlwind Woman went away and the dust
spun around in a circle. Soon Coyote came on her again. "I don't
want you, Whirlwind Woman, go away!" She whirled off. Again
he came on her and he said, "There are some people I like to have
near me, but I do not like you." She flew off but she came back in
his path as he went along the river.

By now Coyote was beginning to like her. "I want you for my
sweetheart," he said to her.

"No," she answered. "I am used to moving all the time. I do
not like to stay in one place. I travel. I would not be the wife for
you."

"You are just like me!" insisted Coyote. "I am always traveling.
I even have the same power you do." Coyote began to run and
turn and spin around, throwing dirt up in the air with his feet and
trying to raise a lot of dust. Whirlwind Woman refused to look
over where he was. Coyote began spinning around again. He

spun and kicked up the dirt and jumped up and down stirring up more dust and kicking it up higher.

"There, you can see I have the same power. You're the wife for me. I'll take you now." He grabbed her and tried to lay down on top of her.

Whirlwind Woman began spinning and she caught Coyote and threw him headfirst into the river bank. Then she blew him into the water so he stuck there in the mud.

"I was only joking. I was not intending to do anything," called Coyote.

But Whirlwind Woman was already far away. "Such is my power," she called back at him.

Coyote Imitates
Mountain Lion

Coyote was going along and he saw a rock rolling down the hill. It rolled down toward some deer and they jumped. Coyote wondered who was rolling stones and looked up at the top of the hill. Another stone came rolling down past Coyote toward the deer and the deer jumped again. Then a third stone came down and the deer jumped only a little. They knew it was only a stone.

The next moment another stone came by Coyote. But this was a soft rock. It was Mountain Lion who had rolled himself up like a rock and was rolling down the hill.

"What a funny rock," thought Coyote. "It doesn't make any noise when it rolls."

Mountain Lion rolled right up to the deer who were not suspicious of the rolling rocks by this time. Then Coyote saw Mountain Lion get up, jump on a big deer and kill it. Mountain Lion picked up the deer and carried it up to a cliff where he could eat it and see the country all around. The rest of the deer ran off around the hill.

Coyote thought this would be a good way to get deer.

He rolled a stone down the hill to where the deer were and they jumped. He rolled another stone and they did not jump as far. When he rolled the third stone they only looked around to see that it was just another stone. Then Coyote rolled himself up in a ball like Mountain Lion and rolled down the hill. When he got there he jumped up and tried to get a deer but he couldn't. He was too dizzy. He just fell over and the deer ran away.

Coyote
and His Knee

Coyote was going along one morning when he saw a good-looking young man out on the prairie.

"Hey, young man, where are you going?" called Coyote.

"I am going out on the war path."

"I am a strong warrior, known by all the people. I can come along and help you."

"You can come along if you are brave."

"Oh, when we meet our enemies you will see. I am the bravest man there is. They will run away when they see me! We will have a good time. We will capture their horses and take whatever they leave behind."

The young man thought this might be Coyote talking but he couldn't be sure. He said, "Come on. You can come."

The warrior told Coyote as they went along that they would camp that night at a place called Scalped Man by the Fire. Coyote didn't like that name.

That afternoon they killed a buffalo and made camp. Coyote made the other man do all the cooking and then Coyote took the best piece of meat for himself, telling the other man that the bravest warriors were always treated like this. Before he went to bed Coyote took all the meat that was left over and packed it around the place where he was sleeping. In case he got hungry he would have the meat right there. He took the liver and spread it out on his chest and put the heart on his knee and fell asleep.

In the middle of the night Coyote heard a noise and raised himself up to look around. Right there in front of him was Scalped Man. Without making a sound Coyote raised his club and brought it down as hard as he could on Scalped Man's head. But it was not Scalped Man, only Coyote's knee with the meat on it and when the club landed Coyote let out a yell. Immediately the other man jumped up.

"What is the matter?"

"It was just Scalped Man. Nothing to worry about now. He came around here but I sent him off."

The other man went back to sleep and Coyote rolled around on the ground holding his knee and trying not to make any noise.

The next morning when they left, the warrior told Coyote they would camp that night at a place called Cooked Meat Flying All Around. Coyote didn't know what to make of that name. As they went along the man saw Coyote's knee was bothering him, causing him to fall behind. Coyote said it would be all right, that he had just hurt it in that fight with Scalped Man.

When they got to camp that night they sat down and waited. When it was dark, meat began flying around them. They caught what they wanted and when they had enough meat the pieces stopped flying around. The warrior said they would camp the next night at the place Where the Arrows Fly Around. Coyote didn't like the name of that place. "I don't know if I can go that far tomorrow. My knee is getting pretty bad you know."

The next day Coyote's knee was really bothering him and he suggested they camp some other place. But the warrior went on. They made camp in a draw where there were some willows and small cottonwoods and made a fire and ate dinner. When it got dark, arrows began flying through the air around them. The warrior stood very still and began to catch the arrows as they came by. Coyote jumped all over trying to dodge them. The more he dodged the closer the arrows came. Finally Coyote got down next to the ground and tried to squeeze into an old badger tunnel. An arrow finally hit him in the arm. He screamed out that he had been killed and rolled over.

The other man came over and kicked his feet and told him to get up. Coyote jumped up and rubbed his eyes.

"What's going on here?" said Coyote. "I must have fallen asleep. This knee is making me very tired."

When they went to bed Coyote said, "You know, you're lucky that Scalped Man didn't go after you when he came into camp. He might have killed you, where he could only wound me."

The warrior told Coyote the next day's camp would be Where the Women Visit the Men. Coyote liked the sound of that place. He said his knee would be much better in the morning and that he could travel very fast the next day if the man wanted to get an early start.

The next morning Coyote did all the cooking and was the first one out on the trail. He kept getting far ahead and he would turn back and yell out, "Hey, can't you keep up? What kind of warrior are you? When we find the enemy I'll have to do all the fighting myself! I have a bad wound and still you can't keep up."

Finally they made camp. After dark two women came into camp. One came over to Coyote but he couldn't tell whether she was young or old. He gave her a piece of meat to eat and he thought by the sound she made that she was very old. He thought younger women would be coming into camp later in the evening so he told her to go away.

When she got up to leave Coyote saw in the firelight that she was a very good-looking young woman and he called out for her to sit down again. But she didn't. Coyote got up and began talking very smoothly, saying she really was very good-looking and that some ghost must have been calling out and telling her to leave. But she just walked off.

At first Coyote thought she might come back or that some other woman would come. But no one came. Coyote then got very angry with himself. He knew the other woman might have spent the night with him. Now he had nothing. It made him so angry he couldn't get to sleep. He could hear the other woman and the warrior talking softly but they weren't making love. He thought for a while that the other man might call out and tell him to come over and make love with this woman. But he didn't call out. Coyote waited until dawn thinking that the other woman might come back, but she never did.

While they were eating breakfast the next morning the other man told Coyote they were going to make camp that night at a place called War Clubs Flying Around. Coyote didn't like the sound of that place so he lagged behind all day saying his knee hurt so much they wouldn't make that camp. But they got there anyway.

When darkness came in Coyote heard the war clubs begin to fly around. The man told Coyote not to dodge them or he would get hit for sure. Coyote dodged them anyway and one hit him on the head and knocked him out. The other man caught two clubs, one for himself and one for Coyote, and then the other clubs stopped flying around. He kicked Coyote and Coyote jumped up and said he must have fallen asleep again. The man told him that they would need these clubs to fight the enemy and gave Coyote one.

While they were eating he said the place they were going the next day was called Vulvas Flying Around. Coyote said right away that his leg was better, that they should leave early and make an early camp. Coyote asked the man whether these were the best kind of vulvas that flew around, very young, just what a man would want. The other man said they were. Coyote asked the man to tell him all about these vulvas but the man went to sleep. Coyote was awake all night thinking about vulvas, what they would be like flying around with no women attached. He wondered how easy they would be to carry around.

Coyote was up early and fixed breakfast and left the man far behind on the trail that day. Coyote kept looking back and shaking his head at how slow the other man was. Coyote thought maybe the man was tired from such a long journey and just couldn't keep up.

After dinner that night it got dark and things began flying around in the camp. Coyote knew what they were and he ran after them trying to grab one, but they stayed just out of his reach, only brushing his fingertips. Coyote ran around until he was almost falling down from exhaustion and then he had an idea. He emptied all the arrows out of his quiver and opened it up like a bag and swung it around trying to catch one of those vulvas. The vulvas all made sweet sounds and Coyote was going crazy with desire. When he came close to grabbing one he could feel that they were just what he wanted. Finally with a tremendous leap Coyote was able to catch one of the flying vulvas in his quiver. He jerked it out and lay down on top of it with a yell as fast as he could—but he couldn't get his member to work at all. The other man was sitting under some trees laughing quietly.

When they went to bed that night the warrior said that the next day they were going to the real place, the place Where the Enemy Attacks.

All the next day Coyote said his knee was bothering him and held back. But the man waited for him. Whenever the man got ahead of him, he would stop and wait for Coyote to catch up. They made camp and went to bed. Coyote's knee hurt all night because he knew they would be attacking in the morning. At dawn when they started off they were surrounded by the enemy right away. Coyote took one look around and ran off, but one of the enemies came after him, killed him and took his scalp. The warrior fought all the other enemies off with his arrows and war club and then went looking for Coyote.

When he found him he kicked him and told him to get up. Coyote jumped up and started running immediately. But he stopped after a short while when he realized no one was chasing him and turned around. "This battle has made me very tired," he cried out to the warrior. "I am going home. Remember, the next time you might have to do this alone. You're lucky I came along." Then Coyote left.

The other man, whose name was White Hawk, went back to his village.

Coyote
Marries His Daughter

Coyote had a stepdaughter. He fell in love with her. One day he got sick. He said to his wife, "I am going to die tomorrow. Don't wrap me up in any blankets, just put me on the hill up there."

The next day, when he was dying, he called his wife and stepdaughter over to him. "If any young man comes around here, make your daughter marry him. He will help you. That is all. I'm sorry I'm going to die."

"I am sorry you are dying. I'll make my daughter marry anyone who comes along."

That night Coyote pretended to be dead. They placed him on the top of the hill, putting a blanket over him, but they did not wrap him up. Then they went home. They cried all that day and that evening.

After sunset someone came along. The daughter said, "My mother, someone is coming along." The old woman said, "You know what your father said. You'll be married to that fellow if he comes here."

Coyote had changed himself to look like a young man. He'd

134

painted himself all up. He went into the woman's lodge.

"What is the matter here my sisters? Why are you crying?"

"I've just lost my husband. I placed him over on the hill."

"What are you people going to do? I feel sorry for you. You ought to get your daughter married so you'll have a son-in-law."

The old woman said, "Coyote, my husband, said that the first man to come along should marry my daughter, so you may have her."

"All right," he said.

The old woman fixed up a tipi for them to live in. The next morning the girl got up before Coyote. She saw in the morning light that there was a scar on his shoulder. She looked close at him. The paint had rubbed off his face. She knew that it was Coyote. She went to her mother's lodge then.

"That's Old Man Coyote in there, that's your husband. I'm not going to stay with him."

"I'm going right over and fix him," said the old woman.

Coyote heard her coming and grabbed his blanket and skipped out.

When she found him gone, she went up to where they'd placed his body. There was only his blanket there. She came back to her lodge. She put some soup on the fire.

"Trick on us," she said to her daughter.

Coyote, Wren and Grouse

Once Coyote was going along and he met Wren. Wren had a small bow and arrows and Coyote began to laugh at this.

"What are you doing? You can't shoot anything with those, my brother. Those arrows won't go very far at all. Your bow is too small."

"Yes, I can shoot far with these," answered Wren. "If you go out to that ridge over there I will shoot you."

Coyote looked out to the ridge and laughed a little. "You can't do this with those little things. That ridge is too far away. Even I can't shoot all the way over there. You are just being foolish. You are too little to be talking like this." He laughed and went on.

A little while later he was walking on that ridge and Fox was following along. Coyote had forgotten all about his talk with Wren. Then he heard a strange sound and looked around to see what it was. Wren's arrow hit him right in the heart. He gave two jumps and fell over dead. Fox pulled out the arrow and jumped over him four times.

"I must have slept for a long time," said Coyote getting up.

"You were not sleeping, you were dead. Wren's arrow struck you in the heart. Why do you fool with Wren? You know he can shoot better than anyone."

Coyote took the arrow from Fox and said, "I will get even with him."

Some time after this Coyote met Wren and proposed a gambling contest. "I have your arrow here. Now you have a chance to win it back." They played a game of throwing arrows. Coyote beat Wren every time, and won all his arrows. Then he won his bow and all his beautiful clothes. Wren was left with almost nothing. Coyote went off singing, "I have won everything from that silly Wren."

Wren began to follow Coyote at some distance.

Coyote came to the lodge of Willow Grouse who had ten young children. Their parents were off hunting. Coyote asked "Who is your father?"

"Flying-past-head."

"No, that cannot be his name. What is the name of your mother?"

"Flying-past-between-the-legs."

"No, that cannot be her name."

He went into the lodge and dug a small hole near the fire. Then he said to the children, "Put some red bearberries into this hole and watch me cook them for you." They did this and crowded around to watch him cook. He pushed the Willow Grouse children into the hole and covered them up with dirt and hot ashes. When they were cooked, he went on.

When the parents came home and found the Grouse children dead, they began to cry. Wren came along and asked why they were crying. They told him they thought Coyote did this.

"I have a grudge against Coyote, too," said Wren. "I want my things back from him. If you can get them back for me I will restore all your children to life."

The Grouse parents flew out after Coyote.

Coyote was then passing along a steep mountain trail. The two Grouse made a detour and came around in front of him. When Coyote came on them, one Grouse flew at his head and Coyote bent over the cliff to avoid him. Then the other one flew between his legs. Coyote lost his balance and fell off the cliff. The Grouse hurried and plucked him as he was falling down. They plucked away his arrows and bow and quiver and clothing and gave these back to Wren. Wren revived all the Grouse children.

Coyote was killed by that fall. Fox found him and jumped over him four times and brought him back to life.

Fox Loses His Tail

Once when Coyote was traveling on the plains he saw two Buffalo bulls. One of the bulls was fat, the other thin.

"At last I see some meat," thought Coyote. "I will walk over there where those bulls are feeding."

"Hey, Grass-eaters," he said, going over to Fat Bull as though he were his friend. "What do you think we ought to do today?"

"We don't know," said Fat Bull.

"Well, I have heard about you. I was told you are good runners. So, I have come to see if you could race."

"No, we can't run well at all," said the bulls.

"Oh, let's race anyway. We will see."

"Well, we have heard you are the best runner. So we don't know if we can run that fast," said Thin Bull.

"Well, let us run against him anyhow," said Fat Bull. "There will be no shame if we are beaten, for he is a good runner."

"You know, I have heard you are very fast runners," said Coyote, "but you are always denying it like this. Let's see who is the best."

"Which way shall we run then?" said Fat Bull who was now anxious to test Coyote. He began to paw the earth a little.

"Over that way, where that hill is," said Coyote, pointing to a place where the sun was going down. He had just come from there and he knew there was a cliff at the top of the hill. No person could run over that cliff and not be killed. A person running a race with the sun in his eyes would not see the cliff when he came to it and would fall right off, unless he knew it was there and could stop in time.

"How far shall we run?" asked Thin Bull.

"Over that hill and down the other side," said Coyote. "Are you ready? All right. Here we go!"

Coyote ran out in front with the bulls right after him, straight into the blinding sun. "I'm very fast," called Coyote back over his shoulder. "You will find this out now." But the bulls were right behind Coyote and anxious to beat him when they got to the foot of the hill. The ground was shaking under their hooves.

"This is steeper than I thought," puffed Coyote, slowing down a little.

The Bulls started to come past him. "I have a lame leg," yelled Coyote. "But I will catch you on the other side near the bottom." He was yelling into the dust for the two Bulls were already past him.

Coyote saw the sun blind the Bulls and watched them run off the top of the hill.

"Ha-ha-ha-ha," laughed Coyote. "I told those two fools I would catch them on the other side. I spoke plainly, but I guess they did not understand me." He trotted around the cliff, down to the bottom. "These persons do not even know their own country. They did not even know this cliff was here. Humph. Well, this fat one will be good for eating. I'll give that skinny one to Raven if he comes along."

The Bulls were both dead. Coyote felt Fat Bull's ribs and smiled but when he looked over at Thin Bull he said, "You wasted your time running. You are too thin for a hunter like me to fool with."

Just as he started butchering he saw a small, gray person coming along. It was One Man, the Kit Fox. "Brother," called Coyote. "Come over here. I have a job for you, and when it is

140

finished, we will both have a good meal. I have plenty of meat."

One Man was very hungry and he asked Coyote what he wanted him to do.

"You see that mountain? I left my Mountain Lion's paw on a rock over there. I will need it to taste the soup with. I can't taste the soup without it."

"That mountain is too far away, Old Man. My moccasins will not last that far and all the way back," protested One Man, smelling Fat Bull.

"Go on, get going," said Coyote. "I have plenty of work to do here to get ready. I will be butchering and making a paunch kettle and gathering wood for a fire and finding roots for the soup, heating stones to boil the meat and everything."

"I will taste the soup. I don't need any Mountain Lion's paw for this," yelled One Man.

"Go! Get out of here!" said Coyote. He was getting very mad. He wanted the Mountain Lion's paw which he was always forgetting and leaving behind.

One Man started toward the mountain but he was afraid Coyote would eat everything up before he came back, so he went only a little ways. Then he came back. "I can't go that far, Old Man. Look how thin my moccasins are." He held up his moccasin to show where his foot was coming through.

"Well, you do the butchering and gather roots and wood and make the paunch kettle and heat the stones. I will get that paw."

One Man watched Coyote disappear in the distance, going toward the mountain. "That Coyote is a bigger fool than I thought," he said to himself. "He has left me here with all this meat. It will take him a few days to get over there and back. I will get fat on this meat and be gone before he gets back to this place."

One Man filled his belly on the fat bull.

A few days later Coyote came back and all the meat was gone. "And I called him brother," said Coyote, looking at the broken bones where One Man had built his fire. "Well, when I catch that One Man person I will call him something besides brother."

He took off on the trail One Man had left and soon came to a river. "He crossed the river here to throw me off the trail," thought Coyote. He smelled along the grass to make sure One

Man had really gone across. Then he saw a patch of rye grass on the other side. "That One Man is foolish enough to be sleeping over there in that bunch of rye grass."

He slipped quietly into the water and swam across and put his nose on the ground again and began looking for One Man. He found the tracks right away. "Just as I thought," said Coyote to himself, "he headed for that rye grass."

Coyote went over and found One Man curled up asleep.

"Now I've got you, you thief," whispered Coyote. "I once called you brother. Now things will be lively for you."

He cut a stick and sharpened one end and pushed it into the ground near the rye grass. He tied One Man's tail to the stick and then got out his fire kit and lit the grass. Flames shot up all over. "Fire! Fire!" shouted Coyote, fanning the flames.

One Man jumped up from his bed and tried to run and something broke. Coyote laughed out loud.

"What have you done to me Old Man?" whimpered One Man, looking at what had happened. His sides were all burned and his tail was gone. "My beautiful tail! Where is it?"

"It's right here on this stick. You were in such a hurry you left it behind," laughed Coyote. "I have punished you for stealing my meat while I went for that Lion's paw. Now listen to me, you thief, you forked-tongue person. I'm going south. You go north, and stop taking things that do not belong to you."

"But my tail, Old Man, what about my tail?"

Coyote took the tail and put it back on One Man's rump.

One Man went up north. He was afraid to go any other way.

Coyote Visits
the Land of the Dead

Coyote and his wife were staying in a nice village. One winter his wife became ill. She died. In time Coyote became very lonely. He did nothing but weep for his wife.

The death spirit came to him and asked if he was crying for his wife.

"Yes, my friend," answered Coyote. "I long for her. There is a great pain in my heart."

After a while the death spirit said, "I can take you to the place where your wife has gone, but if I do, you must do exactly what I say. You can't disregard a single word."

"What would you expect me to do? I will do whatever you say, everything, my friend."

"Well, then let's go."

After they had gone a ways the death spirit again cautioned Coyote to do exactly as he was told and Coyote said he would.

By this time Coyote was having trouble seeing the death spirit. He was like a shadow on an overcast day. They were going across the prairie to the east and the ghost said, "Oh, look at all these

143

horses over there. It must be a roundup." Coyote could not see any horses but he said, "Yes, yes."

They were getting nearer the place of the dead.

"Oh, look at all these service berries! Let's pick some to eat." Coyote could not see the berries, so the ghost said, "When you see me reach up and pull the limb down, you do the same."

The ghost pulled one of the limbs down and Coyote did the same thing. Although he could not see anything, he imitated the ghost, putting his hand to his mouth as though he were eating. He watched how the ghost did everything and imitated him.

"These are very good service berries," said the ghost.

"Yes, it's good we found them."

"Well, let's get going now."

They went on. "We are about to arrive," said the ghost. "Your wife is in a very long lodge, that one over there. Wait here. I will ask someone exactly where."

In a little while the ghost returned and said, "They have told me where your wife is." They walked a short distance. "We are coming to a door here. Do in every way exactly what I do. I will take hold of the door flap, raise it up, and, bending low, will enter. Then you take hold of the door flap and do the same."

In this way they went in. Coyote's wife was right near the entrance. The ghost said, "Sit down here by your wife." They both sat down. "Your wife is now going to prepare some food for us."

Coyote could see nothing. He was sitting in an open prairie where there was nothing in sight. He could barely sense the presence of the shadow.

"Now, she has prepared our food. Let's eat."

The ghost reached down and brought his hand to his mouth. Coyote could see only grass and dust in front of him. They ate. Coyote imitated all the actions of his companion. When they had finished and the woman had apparently put the food away, the ghost said to Coyote, "You stay here. I must go around and see some people. Here we have conditions different from those you have in the land of the living. When it gets dark here it is dawn where you live. When it's dawn for us, it is growing dark for you."

144

Now it was getting dark and Coyote thought he could hear voices, very faintly, talking all around him. Then darkness set in and Coyote could begin to see a little. There were many small fires in the long house. He began to see the people, waking up. They had forms, very vague, like shadows, but he recognized some of them. He saw his wife sitting by his side and he was overjoyed. Coyote went around and greeted all his old friends who had died long ago. This made him very happy. He went among them visiting and talking with everyone. All night he did this. Toward morning he saw a little light around the place where he had entered the long house. The death spirit said to him, "Coyote, our night is falling and in a little while you will not see us. But you must stay here. Do not move. In the evening you will see all these people again."

"Where would I go, my friend? Sure, I will stay right here."

When dawn came Coyote found himself sitting alone in the middle of the prairie. He sat there all day in the heat. He could hear meadowlarks somewhere. It got hotter and he grew very thirsty. Finally evening came and he saw the lodge again. For a couple of days he went on like this, suffering through the daytime in the heat but visiting with his friends every night in the lodge.

One night the death spirit came to him and said, "Coyote, tomorrow you will go home. You will take your wife with you."

"But I like it here very much my friend," Coyote protested. "I am having a good time and should like to remain."

"Yes, but you will go tomorrow. I will advise you about what you are to do. Listen. There are five mountains to the west. You will travel for five days. Your wife will be with you but you must not touch her. Do not yield to any notion you may have to do something foolish. When you have crossed and descended the fifth mountain you can do whatever you want."

"It will be this way, then," said Coyote.

When dawn came, Coyote and his wife set out. At first it seemed to Coyote as though he were alone, but he was aware of his wife's dim presence as she walked along behind. The first day they crossed the first mountain and camped. The next day they crossed the second mountain. They went on like this, camping each night. Each night when they sat across from each other at the fire Coyote could see his wife a little more clearly.

The death spirit had begun to count the days and to figure the distance Coyote had traveled. "I hope he does everything right," he thought, "and takes his wife on to the other world."

The time of their fourth camping was their last camp. On the next day Coyote's wife would become entirely like a living person again. Coyote could see her clearly across the fire now. He could see the light on her face and body but he did not dare to touch her. Suddenly a joyous impulse overtook him. He was so glad to have his wife back! He jumped up and ran around the fire to embrace her.

"Stop! Stop!" screamed his wife. "Coyote do not touch me!"

But her warning had no effect. Coyote rushed to her and just as he touched her she vanished. She disappeared and returned to the shadowland.

When the death spirit learned what Coyote had done he became furious.

"You are always doing things like this, Coyote," he yelled. "I told you not to do anything foolish. You were about to establish the practice of returning from death. Now it won't happen. You have made it this way."

Coyote wept and wept. His sorrow was very deep. He decided that he would go back, he would find the death lodge and find his wife again. He crossed the five mountains. He went out in the prairie and found the place where the ghost had seen the horses, and then he began to do the same things they had done when they were on their way to the shadowland the other time.

"Oh, look at all these horses. It must be a roundup!"

He went on to the place where the ghost had picked the service berries. "Oh, such choice service berries. Let's pick some and eat." He went through the motions of picking and eating the berries. He finally came to the place where the death lodge stood. He said to himself, "Now, when I take hold of the door flap and raise it up you must do the same." Coyote remembered all the things his friend had done and he did them. He saw the spot where he had sat before. He went to it and sat down. "Now your wife has brought us some food. Let's eat." He went through the motions of eating again.

146

Darkness fell and Coyote listened for the voices. He looked all around, but nothing happened. Coyote sat there in the middle of the prairie. He sat there all night but the lodge didn't appear again. In the morning he heard meadowlarks.

Coyote Gets His Head Stuck in an Elk Skull

Coyote was traveling up around Milk River when he heard the sound of the Sun Dance. He stopped and looked all around. He couldn't see anything. "But there must be a camp here," he thought. He wanted very much to dance, but he didn't know where those people were. He stood up on an old elk skull to get a better look around the country, trying to find the place where the sound of dancing was coming from. Suddenly he realized the noise was coming from under his feet.

Coyote got down on the ground and looked through a hole into the skull. He could see some Mouse People holding a Sun Dance. Coyote said to the hole he was looking through, "Get larger!" It grew bigger. As often as he told it to get larger, it did. Finally he was able to get his head inside the skull. The Mouse People ran out as soon as they saw this.

Now Coyote's head was stuck in that elk skull, and he began to cry because he didn't know what to do. He couldn't see where he was going. He yelled at the hole and tried to pull the skull off but it was no use. Finally he wandered off.

Coyote bumped into something with his foot. "Who are you?" he asked.

"I am a cherry tree."

"Good. I must be near the river."

Coyote went on slowly like that, feeling ahead with his feet. If he could find the river he would know which way to go.

He bumped into something again. "Who are you?"

"I am a cottonwood," the tree said to him.

"I must be very near the river now."

Again he felt something with his foot. "Who are you?"

"I am a willow."

"Indeed! I must be right at the river."

Coyote was stepping very carefully now but still he was falling over things. Finally he tripped and fell in the river and the current took him away.

Coyote floated down to where there was a camp and everyone was in swimming. When they saw what was coming they all screamed, "Look out! Look out for that water monster! Get up on the bank!"

When Coyote floated up to where they were he said, "I will give blue beads to the ones who pull me ashore, but they must be young girls. I only allow young girls to touch me."

Two girls went into the river, one on each side, to take hold of his antlers and pull him out. When they got up on the bank Coyote grabbed one of the women and pushed her down and had intercourse with her. When the others saw this they ran back to the village.

"That water monster has violated this woman's virginity!" they all yelled. The mother of the girl ran down to the river with a big stick. Coyote was still having sex with the girl. The mother began beating him with the stick as hard as she could.

Coyote rolled off the girl and said, "Oh, your punishment needs a better stick than this one old woman! Besides, if you want to kill me, the place to hit is not on my back but right here in the middle of my head. The woman got a bigger stick and hit Coyote right in the head and the elk skull broke in two pieces.

When they saw it was Coyote they knew what had happened. Coyote ran off but the women were right behind him.

After a while he got ahead a little and ran behind a hill. He rubbed himself all over with white clay and put on some feathers and laid a white stick across his arm.

When the women came up, he asked what they were doing. When they told him he said, "I saw that Old Man Coyote go by. You should have pounded him to pieces while you had the chance. He's gone now."

Those women were really angry. They wanted to get Coyote.

"Old man," they said, "do you think we can still catch him?"

"No, he's too far ahead now. You should have got him. You know, he's the worst. You should have beaten him up good."

They said, yes, next time they'd do that, and went back to the village.

Coyote
and the Mouse Girls

One time some Mouse Girls were down on the beach and they found a ringed seal. Coyote saw it from a distance at the same time and came running over. The Mouse Girls quickly tried to hide the seal in the sand.

"What have you got there?" said Coyote.

"A stick."

"It has eyes."

"It is a stick with eyes."

"It has flippers."

"It is a stick with flippers."

"It has whiskers."

"It is a stick with whiskers."

Coyote got tired of arguing and pushed them aside. He picked up the ringed seal and went home with it. His wife skinned it and put some of it away and cooked the rest for dinner. When they went to bed there was still some left in the pot.

That night the Mouse Girls sneaked into Coyote's lodge and ate what was left of the seal. Then they defecated in the pot.

The next morning Coyote rolled over and asked his wife to give him some of the seal that was left over. She was half asleep and when she reached in and found nothing but excrement she let out a yell. "Oh, look at this! Look what those Mouse Girls have done! Look at this mess."

Coyote was angry. He said to his wife, "Give me my bow and arrows." He was going out after the Mouse Girls. But she just gave him a small stick and his son's bow. Coyote found the Mouse Girls down by the beach and he ran up to them, notching the stick into his bow. The Mouse Girls huddled together, shuddering, pretending they were frightened. "Oh, Grandfather, we are sorry," they said. "We won't do that again. Please let us louse you."

Coyote thought he might have frightened his granddaughters too much, so he let them louse him. After a while he fell asleep. The Mouse Girls tied a bladder to his buttocks and woke him up.

"Oh, Grandfather, you better go defecate, your belly looks all swollen. Over here is a good dry place."

Coyote went over and defecated but when he turned around to look there was nothing on the ground. Coyote defecated again and heard the sound of its landing but there was nothing on the ground when he turned around.

Coyote went home and told his wife. "A very strange thing has happened to me. I was defecating a while ago. I could hear the sounds when it hit the ground but when I turned around there was nothing there."

"Turn around and let me see," said his wife. When he turned around his wife took a look and said, "Why, you have a big bladder tied up under your anus, that's the trouble."

When he heard this Coyote knew what had happened and he called for his bow and arrows. But his wife just gave him the other things.

Coyote found the Mouse Girls again and they huddled together when they saw him, as though they were afraid. "Oh, Grandfather, we will never do that again. Please. Let us louse you. You will feel much better."

"I have frightened my little granddaughters," he thought to himself. "All right," he said to them, and he lay down.

They began lousing him and he soon fell asleep. They hung red fir tassels over his eyes and woke him up. "Oh, Grandfather, look over there at your house." Coyote looked over. "Hey, my house is on fire!" He ran toward the house as fast as he could, yelling for his wife. His wife came running out but couldn't understand what was wrong with him, why he was jumping all around. Then she looked at Coyote's eyes.

"Come over here," she said. "They have hung fir tassels from your eyebrows."

"I am going to kill those Mouse Girls. Give me my bow and arrows." But his wife just gave him the stick and the child's bow.

Coyote found the girls again and was all ready to shoot them, but they spoke softly and said they would be good and asked to louse him. Coyote said it would be all right but that he didn't want any tricks.

Coyote lay down and after a while he fell asleep. The Mouse Girls tatooed his face and changed his hair all around so he looked like a woman and then woke him up. "Grandfather, you look pale. You should go down to the stream and get a drink."

Coyote went down to the stream and when he saw his reflection he thought he was seeing one of the beautiful women of the Caribou People. He told her not to move. He said he was going to marry her right away and that she should wait there while he ran home and got his things and came back to live with her.

When he got home, Coyote gathered up everything he owned and piled it all up outside his lodge. When he had it all together he lifted the load up to his shoulders. It was an enormous pile. He could hardly be seen underneath it.

"Where are you going with all that?" said his wife.

"I am going to live with a different woman. I have met a beautiful young woman of the Caribou People and I am going to marry her."

"Is that why you have painted yourself up?"

"What do you mean?"

"You have done something to your face and turned your hair all around. You look ugly."

"You are just jealous! I am leaving."

Coyote could barely move under the staggering load of posses-

153

sions and he stumbled down the trail bumping into trees all the way to the stream. When he looked into the water again he saw the woman. He told her that he was going to give her all his things and he began throwing everything he owned into the stream. Some of the things sank and he was glad to see her taking these things, but some things floated away and he got very angry with her when he saw this.

"Who do you think you are, throwing my presents away like this?" said Coyote and he jumped into the stream to get closer to the woman. But as soon as he jumped in his legs got tangled up in the huge pile of things he had thrown in and then his arms got bound up in something and he drowned.

A few days later Coyote washed up on the beach. Some people came along and brought him back to life. They took him home. In those days you found Coyote like that all the time.

Coyote Avenges His Death

Once Coyote was coming up a long river and at the head of the valley he climbed up on a ridge and looked around. Down below he could see a man jumping back and forth over a deep ravine. The man had only one leg. He had tied his other leg to his back.

Coyote was on his way to a meeting where there would be many powerful shamans and he thought this would be a good trick to do. They would all ask him how he did it, but he wouldn't tell anyone.

He went down closer to watch the man jump the ravine, thinking he might be able to see how he did it, and not have to pay the man to learn how to do the trick. While he was watching, the man stumbled and fell down to the bottom of the ravine. He got up and was very mad.

"Someone has been watching me," he thought. "This is why I fell. Someone is trying to steal my power." He put his other leg on and climbed out of the ravine. When he got to the top he saw Coyote waiting. "I thought so!" he said and he grabbed Coyote and hurled him into the ravine. The fall killed Coyote and the man came down and threw him in the river.

Coyote floated along until his body rolled up on the shore in some wire grass. Magpie saw him and came over. "Someone has killed Coyote," said Magpie. "I've always wondered if he had good brow fat." Magpie began pecking at Coyote's head.

"What are you doing?" yelled Coyote, jumping up. "Are you crazy? I was asleep here in the sun and you come along and begin pecking at my head. I have just brought the daughter of the chief of this place safely across this river. If you knew who I was you wouldn't be pecking at me like that."

"How could you have done this?" said Magpie. "You were dead. That man threw you in the river after he killed you. You weren't carrying anyone across the river," said Magpie, flying away.

Right away Coyote defecated and turned around to address his excrement. "What has happened?" he asked. "Tell me how I got here." The excrement said, "Up above here a powerful man killed you. You will have to avenge your death. You will have to kill him."

Coyote kicked sand over his excrement and went back up the river. When he got to the place where he died, he climbed up to the top of the ravine. The man who had one leg tied to his back was jumping back and forth. Coyote hid in the trees and watched him. After a while he made him stumble and the man fell to his death.

Coyote went on his way.

The Hoodwinked Dancers

Once Coyote was coming along through the bulrushes on the edge of a lake and he stopped to take a look around. There were all kinds of water birds there, including mallard ducks and those big white swans. They were camping there and they were swimming all around. There were a lot of good-looking fat geese.

Coyote came out of the bulrushes and began walking along where everyone would see him. He had a big bag of some sort on his back.

"Hey, Coyote," they called. "What are you carrying in there? It looks heavy."

"Oh, these are my songs."

"Why do you have so many songs?"

"I have many visions. I get all these songs that way. Besides, I like to dance, so I like to have a lot of songs with me."

"Well, let's have a big dance then. You can sing some of these songs."

"Well, okay. But these are powerful songs. You can't fool around. You have to do what I say. You can't act crazy."

They said they would be good and they made up a big place for dancing.

Coyote began to tell them what to do. He took out his dancing sticks.

"No one may look at anything while I am singing my songs. You must dance with your eyes shut. If you open your eyes you'll get hurt bad, maybe even killed."

They agreed to keep their eyes shut and they began to dance. Coyote was a good singer and they danced hard. Coyote was beating on a log with his dancing sticks.

"Remember, brothers, keep your eyes closed. When we are finished maybe I will see about giving you some of these songs."

While they were all dancing around, Coyote reached into his bag and pulled out a big club. When one fat duck came by he hit it over the head and killed it.

"Stop brothers!" yelled Coyote. "Look at this! Look at what has happened to this person. He opened his eyes and now he is dead. Keep your eyes closed."

They all began dancing again and even singing some of their own songs, dancing as hard as they could. Coyote grabbed one of the ducks by the throat and it made a bad squawking noise. "That's right brothers, sing as loud as you can."

He'd hit almost all the ducks with his club when a black duck who had been listening to all these noises opened up one eye, only a little. He saw what Coyote was doing and called out to the others, "Run away! This is Coyote hitting everyone with a stick." The birds that were left ran for the water but only a few got away.

Coyote
Swallows Horned Toad

Wildcat and Coyote were sitting on a hill having a talk about
how each got his food. There was a narrow strip of rain out in the
valley and Coyote said, "Places where it rains like that we call
'lying on its back.' There is usually a cornfield at those places.
Let's go over there."

There was a corn patch at that place that belonged to Horned
Toad. Coyote told Wildcat to hide in the bushes and he would go
down and look over things. When he came back he said, "That's
good corn down there, but we have to be careful. Horned Toad is
dangerous."

About midnight they went down and ate the corn. Horned
Toad heard them eating and ran out and chased them away. This
happened for three nights. On the fourth night, Wildcat didn't
get away. He was killed.

The next day Coyote went to see Horned Toad. Coyote
changed the way he looked so Horned Toad wouldn't recognize
him.

"Cousin," said Coyote, "you certainly raise a lot of corn. I raise corn, too." He told Horned Toad where his corn patch was and that he had someone taking care of it for him. "I am glad I have a man watching it for me. It is very bad when someone gets into your cornfield and steals corn."

"This is true," said Horned Toad. "The only way to get corn is to come and ask for it."

"Yes, that's the way it goes," said Coyote.

Horned Toad went out to get some corn. He cooked it up for himself and Coyote. Coyote asked for a second meal and Horned Toad cooked up some more corn. Then Coyote asked for a third meal, but Horned Toad wouldn't give him anymore.

Coyote asked four times. Each time Horned Toad said, "No." Each time he refused, Coyote said, "If you do not get some more corn for me I will swallow you up." The fourth time Horned Toad said, "Go ahead and swallow me."

Coyote swallowed Horned Toad, then he went out into Horned Toad's corn patch for more corn. He looked up and saw birds circling around and thought they might be after the corn. "Go away. I have worked very hard on this field," yelled Coyote.

Then Coyote went back to Horned Toad's house and lay down for a nap. While he was sleeping, Horned Toad began moving around inside him. Coyote woke up. "Those young ears of corn are like this," said Coyote. "They give you a stomachache." Coyote went out and tried to defecate but he couldn't.

He came in and went to sleep again. While he was asleep, Horned Toad made a noise—pssszz. Coyote jumped up and looked around. Horned Toad went "pssszz" four times. On the fourth time, Coyote said, "It is always like this when someone dies. The spirits come back and make a noise like this."

Then Horned Toad began to talk. "What's this?" he asked, grabbing Coyote's stomach.

Coyote answered, "That's my stomach."

Horned Toad went all through Coyote's intestines like that, asking what they were. At last Horned Toad came to Coyote's heart. "What's this?" he asked.

"That is my heart."

Horned Toad took one of his knives and cut a cross on Coyote's heart. Coyote jumped up and fell over dead.

160

Horned Toad had asked Coyote all of these questions so he could find his way out. He came out Coyote's anus and went back to work in his corn patch.

Coyote Visits the Women

One time Coyote was walking along the edge of a big lake. He wanted to cross over to an island on the other side but he did not know how to swim. He was thinking of how he might get over there when he noticed a young man paddling a canoe. When he got closer Coyote called him over to the shore and asked what he was doing. "I am hunting ducks."

"Very well. I will paddle your canoe for you while you are shooting."

The young man agreed and they proceeded out onto the lake together. After they had gotten some ducks Coyote said, "Brother, let me go across to the other side there while you are plucking these ducks." The other man agreed and went ashore and Coyote paddled over to the island and tied the canoe up and climbed a hill so he could look around. He saw a large village, a circle of forty lodges with one in the center. He went up to the village and at the edge he met a young girl. Coyote thought she was good-looking. "Are there many men here?" asked Coyote.

"We don't know what men are."

"Who lives in the center of the circle?"

"Two chief women who look after us. Go to them, they are our leaders."

Coyote entered the main lodge. On the right there was a young fox strapped to a papoose board and on the other side there was a rabbit. The rabbit jumped up and hit Coyote with a coup stick which meant that Coyote would belong to the rabbit's mother.

Rabbit Woman sat down next to Coyote and handed him a bowl of pemmican to eat. When he was through eating he handed her the bowl and asked, "What are these two here for?"

"These are our children."

"Are there any men?"

"No, we don't know what men are."

The lodge was beautifully decorated with skins and quill and bead work. There were all kinds of nice work bags around. Coyote thought he might have some fun and get some of these things for himself. He thought, "I will show them something." He showed them his erect member making his pants stand up. Rabbit Woman noticed it first and stooped down to look at it more closely. She was amazed. The other woman also looked down. "What is this thing, what is it good for?"

"For connecting our bodies together."

"Is it necessary to put this in some part of my body?"

"Come over here, I will show you."

He put his hand under the woman's dress and indicated a place. "If I put my member in this place, you will find it very agreeable." Coyote eased her down on the earth and began to have intercourse with her. When he was finished he made love with her a second time and then rolled over and said to the other, "I would like to lay your legs open like this too." He got on top of her. During the time he was with this woman, the mother of all the women in the village came along. She heard the women making agreeable sounds and wanted to know how pleasurable this intercourse was. Coyote took her down and had coitus with her until his penis went flat. But she wanted more and made him do it again. It wouldn't work and Coyote was afraid. All the other young women were crowding around and demanding to have intercourse with Coyote. Coyote couldn't get his member erect.

They were all grabbing for it and trying to make it stiff. Coyote wanted to get away and he started to move off but they grabbed him.

"After intercourse," he warned them, "you will be heavy, bringing forth children, who will come out of that opening." They did not want to believe him. "You will give birth to little boys and girls. The boys will have a member hanging down like this. You will have all you want."

Coyote saw that they didn't believe him. They wanted intercourse. He wanted to get away. "I have to go off and pass water," he said. "It is not possible for you to watch while I do this." But the women wanted to go along so he wouldn't get away. "I won't go away," said Coyote. "I will be on top of that hill there. You can see me. It is impossible for me to run while I am passing water anyway."

Coyote went up to the top of the hill and as soon as he got to the top he ran for the canoe. One woman saw him fleeing and gave the alarm. They came after him but he reached the canoe first. Some of the women jumped into the water and tried to swim after him but he paddled off as hard as he could.

When he got to the other side he told his companion, "Brother, there was nothing over there but rocks and trees. I found nothing."

The women watched the men on the far shore until they disappeared.

Coyote Gambles

One time Coyote went out trying to find someone to gamble with but there was no one in any of the camps. An old woman told him that everyone had gone over to the coast to gamble. Coyote went home and did his gambling spirit power ceremony. That took five days. Then he went over to the coast.

On the way over he came to a house where two women were living. They begged Coyote to stay and be their man but he said he was going gambling. They wanted to be with Coyote so badly they followed him over to the coast. On the way they explained that the gambling game over there was not like the Stick game they played over where Coyote lived. They told him how it worked. It was a game played with dead people's bones.

When Coyote came over there he said, "Hey, who wants to play the Stick game?" Sea Lion said, "We don't play that over here, we do it a different way." Coyote said he didn't know how to play the other game. "My power is no good for that," he said. He lit his pipe and sat off by himself. Elk came over and said,

"Coyote, get in this game. You'll win." Coyote said, "No, I would lose everything, I'm no good at that."

Otter came over to where Coyote was smoking. "You play that Stick game pretty well, Coyote. You should try this." Otter thought Coyote would lose but he didn't tell him this.

Finally, after everyone told him he would do fine, Coyote agreed to play the Dead Bones game. But he asked them not to make the betting too high because he wouldn't win this kind of game. He was playing only as a favor to them.

Coyote played with Beaver first. The bet was five slaves. Coyote won. Everyone laughed at this luck. Otter was next. Coyote won ten slaves. They all laughed. Deer played next and lost twenty slaves. They were not all laughing now. Coyote beat Elk and Seal. When it was Sea Lion's turn he tried to talk Coyote out of playing. Coyote said it was no good to quit, a person should be allowed to win a little before quitting. Sea Lion said this was true, but that Coyote was winning everything. Coyote finally agreed to quit.

"Next time I come over here, though, I want to play the Stick game," said Coyote, "not this game with dead people's bones. I can't win anything at this kind of game."

He took what he had won and went inland with the two women.

Woodpecker Feeds Coyote

Coyote was living in a big village.

"Oh Grandmother," he said one day, "I wonder where that younger brother of mine dwells."

"Who is that?" said his grandmother.

"Oh, you know, Woodpecker."

"Why, yes, of course. There is a certain point over near some hills in that direction where the river starts. In that place all the trees grow up close to the river and there is good bottomland. That's the place where he lives."

"So that's where it is. I can't see that dwelling from here, but I suppose that's where he lives. I think I might as well go over and pay him a visit."

"That's the way," said his grandmother. "Your aunts and uncles are always doing this kind of visiting."

So Coyote went over to where the trees grew at the head of that river. He found Woodpecker's house and went inside.

"Hey, my brother, what a pleasant surprise," called Woodpecker.

"I haven't come for anything in particular," said Coyote, looking around. "I merely happened to think of you all of a sudden. 'Why, I think I'll go over and visit my brother Woodpecker!' is what I thought."

"Well, I wonder what I can give you to eat. We haven't any food right now. I'll have to hunt something up." Woodpecker called out to his wife, "My wife, where is that gathering skin?" She gave it to him and he set out.

He went out into the woods to the place where a great tree was. He landed on the side and began to thump it to see what sort of sound it made. He moved up the side like that, thumping, until he heard a sound he liked. Then he began to peck a hole, because this was where the honey was. It was beautiful honey and when he got a good flow going he spread his gathering skin on the ground to catch it. After he got a good supply he stopped the flow and dropped back to the ground. Then he tied up his bundle and started for home.

When he arrived at the place where he and his wife lived, he went inside. He put the honey in a wooden bowl and put it in front of Coyote. "There, my brother, go right ahead and eat this."

Coyote was so delighted with the sweet taste that he ate the whole thing up. "Oh, I don't think I've been this full in a long time. And say, my brother, I should be starting on my way now. I think our grandmother is looking for me. I told her I would be back early."

So Coyote left and went back to the place where he lived and went inside.

"So, you have come back," said his grandmother. "Did you really see your brother Woodpecker?"

"Oh yes, Grandmother, and I'll tell you, he gave me something to eat that was delicious."

"What is that?"

"Honey, that's what it was. It was in a big wooden bowl filled right up to the brim. You may not believe it, but I ate up every bit of that honey it was so good."

"That's the way with your uncles and your aunts when they go to visit one another. They give each other the best of whatever they have. They are good to each other like that. They talk a lot.

Did you have a good talk with your brother?"

"Oh, yes, we talked a lot over that honey."

"That's good."

Coyote
and the Mallard Ducks

Coyote was traveling up the river when he saw five Mallard Duck girls swimming on the other side. He hid himself in the bushes and became aroused right away. Then he thought out a plan to satisfy himself.

Coyote lengthened his penis and let it fall into the river. It floated on top of the water. Coyote didn't like this, so he pulled it back in and tied a rock to it to keep it below the surface of the water. He threw his penis back in and it went straight to the bottom. With much pain he pulled his penis back in and tied a smaller rock to it. This was just right. It floated just below the surface of the water where no one could see it. He sent it across to where the girls were swimming. He began copulating with the oldest girl.

Now, these girls did not know what was wrong with their older sister, the way she was moving around in the water and making strange sounds. Then they saw what was happening and they grabbed the penis and tried to pull it out. When they couldn't, they got out on the bank and held down their older sister and tried to pull it out that way, but they couldn't and they began laughing about it.

When Coyote had satisfied himself he called over to the girls and said, "My sisters, what is the problem over there?" They told him. He said, "Cut that thing off with some wire grass." They did, and Coyote cut the other end off where he was and the middle section of the penis fell in the river and became a ledge.

The eldest girl became ill then. Coyote went down the river a short distance, swam across and then came upstream to the girls' camp where the oldest girl was almost dead.

The girls recognized Coyote and said, "Coyote, the medicine man, has come." They asked him to cure the sick girl. He told them he would do it, but they had to close up all the chinks in the lodge so no one could see in and steal his medicine by watching. He told them to leave him alone with the girl for a while.

He got the sisters together around the lodge and told them to sing a song and keep time on a log with sticks. "Keep time on the log very carefully, for now I am going to take it out."

Coyote began singing, "I will stick it back on, I will stick it back on."

He went into the lodge and copulated again with the Mallard Duck girl and recovered the end of his penis. The girl was cured.

After that everyone said the medicine of Coyote was very powerful.

Coyote
Steals Otter's Coat

One time the animals decided to have a council to see who had the finest fur. They all had different coats, some with short hair, some with long, some with spots, some colored yellow or black, some brown. They were always arguing about whose coat was best.

All the animals had heard that Otter had the finest coat but no one knew because Otter lived up at the head of a long creek and never came down to where the other animals were. They did not even know exactly where he lived, but only the general direction. They hoped he would come. They thought he would hear about the council from someone and come along.

Coyote had been listening to all this talk. He thought his own coat was the finest but he was worried that some of the others might think Otter's was better. He could see them deciding that way, so he began asking about where Otter lived. When someone gave him an answer, he would look away like he wasn't listening so no one would know what he was thinking.

Then, without saying anything, he went off to find Otter.

He walked up the creek for four days and found him. He knew it was Otter right away because Otter's fur was soft, dark brown and very thick.

Otter was glad to see him. "Coyote, where are you going?"

"The animals sent me up to bring you down to the council. Because you live so far away, they thought you would not know the road."

This pleased Otter very much. They set off right away for the village.

They traveled all day and when night came Coyote found a place to camp. The country was strange to Otter. Coyote cut down some bushes for beds and fixed up everything.

The next morning they set off again. Late in the afternoon Coyote began collecting sticks along the way.

"What are you doing, brother?" asked Otter.

"We'll make a good fire tonight and sleep warm and comfortable."

After a while, when it was near sunset, they stopped and made camp.

When supper was over Coyote got out a stick and carved it into a paddle.

"What are you making there?"

"This is a paddle. I always have good dreams when I sleep with a paddle under my head."

When he was finished with the paddle, Coyote cut away all the bushes to make a clear path down to the river.

"What are you doing?"

"This place is called 'the place where it rains fire.' Sometimes it rains fire here. The sky looks this way tonight. You go to sleep. I'll sit up and watch. If the fire comes, as soon as you hear me shout, run down this path and jump in the river. You better hang your coat on that limb over there so it won't get burned."

The Otter hung his coat up and went to sleep.

After a while, Coyote called out in a low voice to see if Otter was awake. There was no answer. He called out again. Otter was really sleeping. Then Coyote took the paddle and loaded it up with hot coals from the fire. He threw them up into the air and shouted, "It's raining fire! It's raining fire!"

The hot coals were falling everywhere and Otter jumped up and ran for the river. "Jump in the water and swim!" yelled Coyote, who was right behind him. Otter jumped in and swam out into the middle of the river. Finally the fire stopped falling down. Otter called out after Coyote. There was no answer.

Coyote went down to the council with Otter's coat on. When the other animals saw him they thought it was Otter and agreed Otter had a very fine coat. They were all anxious to meet him, but Otter was very bashful. He kept his arm up over his face. Finally Bear pulled his arm away and they saw it was only Coyote. Bear tried to grab him, but Coyote was too quick. He got away.

Coyote and Buzzard

Coyote was lying down under a tree after a big rainstorm. Up in the sky he could see a fine rainbow coming out. It covered the whole sky. "I wonder if I could get up there," he thought. "Those colors would make fine paints for my arrows."

Just then he saw Buzzard. "Oh, Uncle, come over here. I would like you to take me up there where I can get at some of that arrow paint."

"All right, my nephew, I'll take you up there. I go up there a lot. Get on my back."

Coyote climbed up on Buzzard's back where he could hold on to his wings. Buzzard took off and they flew like that for a long time. Finally they got to the edge of the sky.

"You stay here, my nephew. I will go after that arrow paint for you."

Coyote was hanging on to the edge of the sky. He was there for a long time. "My uncle," he called out. But he didn't hear anything. He began to whistle. "My uncle!" He made a lot of noise, but he didn't see anyone. After a while he couldn't hang on any longer and fell. He fell for two moons, down and down toward the ground. When he came to the earth he fell into a hollow tree where he couldn't get out.

An old woman was coming along and she came over to this tree to cut some wood. While she chopped, she opened up a hole in the side of the tree and saw some pubic hairs sticking out. When she saw those she said to herself, "Oh, a bear is in there." She pulled out one of the hairs and ran back to the village with it. When she got there she showed it to her husband. "Oh, this is bear hair, sure enough," said the old man.

He grabbed his bow and arrows and they walked out to where the tree was. The woman began chopping again and the man stood ready to shoot. Suddenly they heard a voice say, "My aunt, make a bigger hole."

"Oh, it's Coyote in there," said the old woman, and she chopped a bigger hole.

When he got out Coyote thanked the old woman.

"We thought it was a bear in there," said the old man. "We needed that meat."

Coyote kicked the tree and said, "Come out, bear!" A bear came out of the tree and Coyote killed it. He gave it to the man and his wife and left.

He went off thinking, "I wonder what happened to Buzzard."

Coyote Takes Water
from the Frog People

Coyote was out hunting and he found a dead deer. One of the
deer's rib bones looked just like a big dentalia shell and Coyote
picked it up and took it with him. He went up to see the Frog
People. The Frog People had all the water. When anyone wanted
any water to drink or cook with or to wash, they had to go and get
it from the Frog People.

Coyote came up. "Hey, Frog People. I have a big dentalia shell.
I want a big drink of water. I want to drink for a long time."

"Give us that shell," said the Frog People, "and you can drink
all you want."

Coyote gave them the shell and began drinking. The water was
behind a large dam where Coyote drank.

"I'm going to keep my head down for a long time," said
Coyote, "because I'm really thirsty. Don't worry about me."

"Okay, we won't worry," said the Frog People.

Coyote began drinking. He drank for a long time. Finally one of
the Frog People said, "Hey, Coyote, you sure are drinking a lot of
water there. What are you doing that for?"

Coyote brought his head up out of the water. "I'm thirsty."

"Oh."

After a while one of the Frog People said, "Coyote, you sure are drinking a lot of water. Maybe you better give us another shell."

"Just let me finish this drink," said Coyote, putting his head back underwater.

The Frog People wondered how a person could drink so much water. They didn't like this. They thought Coyote might be doing something.

Coyote was digging out under the dam all the time he had his head underwater. When he was finished he stood up and said, "That was a good drink. That was just what I needed."

Then the dam collapsed and the water went out into the valley and made the creeks and rivers and waterfalls.

The Frog People were very angry.

"You have taken all the water Coyote!"

"It is not right that one people have all the water. Now it is where everyone can have it."

Coyote did that. Now anyone can go down to the river and get a drink of water or some water to cook with or just swim around.

Coyote Finishes His Work

From the very beginning, Coyote was traveling around all over the earth. He did many wonderful things when he went along. He killed the monsters and the evil spirits that preyed on the people. He made the Indians, and put them out in tribes all over the world because Old Man Above wanted the earth to be inhabited all over, not just in one or two places.

He gave all the people different names and taught them different languages. This is why Indians live all over the country now and speak in different ways.

He taught the people how to eat and how to hunt the buffalo and catch eagles. He taught them what roots to eat and how to make a good lodge and what to wear. He taught them how to dance. Sometimes he made mistakes, and even though he was wise and powerful, he did many foolish things. But that was his way.

Coyote liked to play tricks. He thought about himself all the time, and told everyone he was a great warrior, but he was not. Sometimes he would go too far with some trick and get someone

179

killed. Other times, he would have a trick played on himself by someone else. He got killed this way so many times that Fox and the birds got tired of bringing him back to life. Another way he got in trouble was trying to do what someone else did. This is how he came to be called Imitator.

Coyote was ugly too. The girls did not like him. But he was smart. He could change himself around and trick the women. Coyote got the girls when he wanted.

One time, Coyote had done everything he could think of and was traveling from one place to another place, looking for other things that needed to be done. Old Man saw him going along and said to himself, "Coyote has now done almost everything he is capable of doing. His work is almost done. It is time to bring him back to the place where he started."

So Great Spirit came down and traveled in the shape of an old man. He met Coyote. Coyote said, "I am Coyote. Who are you?"

Old Man said, "I am Chief of the earth. It was I who sent you to set the world right."

"No," Coyote said, "you never sent me. I don't know you. If you are the Chief, take that lake over there and move it to the side of that mountain."

"No. If you are Coyote, let me see you do it."

Coyote did it.

"Now, move it back."

Coyote tried, but he could not do it. He thought this was strange. He tried again, but he could not do it.

Chief moved the lake back.

Coyote said, "Now I know you are the Chief."

Old Man said, "Your work is finished, Coyote. You have traveled far and done much good. Now you will go to where I have prepared a home for you."

Then Coyote disappeared. Now no one knows where he is anymore.

Old Man got ready to leave, too. He said to the Indians, "I will send messages to the earth by the spirits of the people who reach me but whose time to die has not yet come. They will carry messages to you from time to time. When their spirits come back into their bodies, they will revive and tell you their experiences.

"Coyote and myself, we will not be seen again until Earth-woman is very old. Then we shall return to earth, for it will require a change by that time. Coyote will come along first, and when you see him you will know I am coming. When I come along, all the spirits of the dead will be with me. There will be no more Other Side Camp. All the people will live together. Earth-mother will go back to her first shape and live as a mother among her children. Then things will be made right."

Now they are waiting for Coyote.

Bibliographic Note

In preparing this collection I researched material primarily in four publications: the *Journal of American Folklore*, *Memoirs of the American Folklore Society*, *Anthropological Papers of the American Museum of Natural History*, and *Publications of the Jesup North Pacific Expedition*. I also examined stories in the series of *Bulletins* and *Annual Reports* issued by the Bureau of American Ethnology, and the series of monographs published by the American Ethnological Society. Other important sources included publications of the Field Museum of Natural History in Chicago, the Carnegie Institution, Columbia University, the Smithsonian Institution, and the University of California at Berkeley. (Permission to use these derived sources for adaption was obtained from publishers as a matter of courtesy.)

In addition to these collections, I made use of a number of general works on native Americans for background, among them *The Lost Universe* by Gene Weltfish, *Indians of the Plains* by Robert Lowie, *Blackfoot Lodge Tales* by George Bird Grinnell, *Cultures of the Pacific Northwest Coast* by Philip Drucker, *The Sacred Pipe* by Joseph Epes Brown, *The Navajo* by Clyde Kluckhohn and Dorothea Leighton, and *Seeing With a Native Eye*, edited by Walter Capps.

The reader interested in pursuing a study of the hero-trickster figure in American Indian mythology should examine Paul Radin's *The Trickster* (the 1972 Schocken paperback edition of which includes the material by

Diamond and Jung mentioned in my Introduction) and Stith Thompson's *Tales of the North American Indians* for its comparative notes and bibliography. Franz Boas discusses trickster and transformer motifs in an essay in the *Thirty-First Annual Report of the Bureau of American Ethnology*, and Archie Phinney provides a short but interesting essay on the effect of outside influence on trickster stories in his introduction to *Nez Perce Texts*. The way in which a storyteller communicates a Coyote story to his audience is the subject of an article by J. Barre Toelken, "The 'Pretty Languages' of Yellowman: Genre, Mode and Texture in Navajo Coyote Narratives" in *Genre*, vol. 2, no. 3 (University of Illinois at Chicago Circle, September, 1969). "Coyote Tales: A Paiute Commentary" by Judy Trejo in the *Journal of American Folklore*, vol. 87, no. 343, is also recommended, as is an article by Dell Hymes, "Folklore's Nature and the Sun's Myth," in the *Journal of American Folklore*, vol. 88, no. 350, for what it has to say about the special problems of translating native American oral literature. In "The Incredible Survival of Coyote" (in *The Old Ways*, City Lights Books, 1977), Gary Snyder examines Coyote's influence on modern poetry.

Readers interested in more peripheral materials might want to examine J. Frank Dobie's extensive, annotated references in *The Voice of the Coyote* and Lillian Barclay's wide-ranging bibliography on coyotes, some of which pertains to Coyote, in *Publications of the Texas Folklore Society*, no. 14.

Finding any single Coyote story in various extant collections remains difficult. Few attempts have been made to codify North American Indian narratives, or to cross-reference them so a reader could, if he wanted, locate ninety or so versions of "The Eye-juggler" incident, or compare the creation myths of tribes living in different parts of the country. Remedios Wycoco's "The Types of North American Indian Tales" (unpublished doctoral dissertation, Indian University, 1951), was developed specifically as an aid to classifying native American tales but it has a limited circulation. Stith Thompson's *Motif-Index of Folk-Literature* has some application. The most useful, widely available cross-index for locating trickster stories is the comparative notes section of Thompson's *Tales of the North American Indians.* Boas cross-indexed about two hundred incidents in the trickster cycle, primarily in Pacific Northwest Coast stories, in *Thirty-First Annual Report of the Bureau of American Ethnology.* The special problems of classifying these narratives is the subject of Alan Dundes's "The Morphology of North American Indian Folktales" in *Folklore Fellows Communications,* vol. 81, no. 195. Dundes discusses the peculiar prejudice of folklorists historically to dismiss, as one Englishman put it, Indian narratives as "formless and void, bearing the same relationship to good European fairy tales as the invertebrates do to the vertebrate kingdom in the animal world."

This note would not be complete without mention of some other Coyote collections. *Old Man Coyote* by Frank Linderman, *Coyote Stories* by Mourning Dove, *Old Man Coyote* by Clara Kern Bayliss, *Coyote Tales* by Hildegard Thompson, and *Old Indian Legends*, a collection of Sioux trickster stories by Gertrude Bonnin, are all, I believe, out of print. Alice Marriott's *Saynday's People,* originally published as *Winter-Telling Stories,* Newell Lion's *Penobscot Transformer Tales, Nu Mee Poom Tit Wah Tit* (Nez Perce legends by the Nez Perce Tribe), and *Coyote Stories* by Robert A. Roessel and Dillon Platero, a Navajo publication, are in print. Jarold Ramsey's *Coyote Was Going There: Indian Literature of the Oregon Country* is new. Although not a collection strictly speaking, Barry Gifford's *Coyote Tantras,* a series of poems on the nature of the character, is worthy of mention.

I wish to express a debt of gratitude to the following people in particular: Alfred Kroeber, James Mooney, James W. Schultz, Robert Lowie, George Bird Grinnell, Mari Sandoz, William Wildschut, Morris Edward Opler, George Dorsey, Clark Wissler, Frank Boas, James Tiet, Frank Linderman, Stephan Powers, Frank Hamilton Cushing, John Ewers, Elsie Clews Parsons, Archie Phinney and Melville

Jacobs. It is through their efforts that much of this source material and its cultural context has been preserved, and it is to them that this book is in part a tribute.

Barry Holstun Lopez, who "belongs at the forefront of a growing cadre of wilderness writers like John McPhee and Edward Abbey," *(Los Angeles Times)* is the acclaimed author of OF WOLVES AND MEN.

RIVER NOTES:
The Dance of Herons 52514 $2.25

"A prose poem, a love song to a mountain river, an almost primeval prayer to the glorious power of nature...a heady distillation of everything that is mystical yet comforting in the mountains around us." *Denver Post* "An abundance of rewards and revelations...I think I will never again stand on the bank of any river and watch the water in quite the same way." *Chicago Tribune*

DESERT NOTES:
Reflections in The Eye of a Raven 53819 $2.25

In this collection of narrative contemplation, naturalist Lopez invites the reader to discover the beauty of the desert. "A magic evocation, Castenda purged of chemistry and trappings...one of the most sensitive and lyrical evocations of nature." *Publishers Weekly*

GIVING BIRTH TO THUNDER, SLEEPING WITH HIS DAUGHTER
54551 $2.95

In 68 tales from 42 American Indian tribes, Lopez recreates the timeless adventures and rueful wisdom of Old Man Coyote, an American Indian hero with a thousand faces—and a thousand tricks. "A rich sampling of Coyote tales to be read for entertainment...a different, lighthearted side of Indian culture." *Publishers Weekly*